John Adams

IN HIS OWN WORDS

John Adams

EDITED BY ROBERT C. BARON

In association with the
Boston Public Library

FULCRUM
GOLDEN, COLORADO

Library of Congress Cataloging-in-Publication Data

Adams, John, 1735-1826.
John Adams, in his own words / edited by Robert C. Baron.
    p. cm. -- (Speaker's corner)
Includes bibliographical references.
ISBN 978-1-55591-712-8 (pbk.)
1. Adams, John, 1735-1826--Quotations. 2. Adams, John, 1735-1826--Correspondence. 3. Adams, John, 1735-1826--Political and social views. 4. Adams, John, 1735-1826--Philosophy. 5. Adams, John, 1735-1826--Knowledge and learning. 6. United States--Politics and government--1775-1783--Sources. 7. United States--Politics and government--1783-1809--Sources. 8. United States--Intellectual life--18th century--Sources. 9. United States--Intellectual life--19th century--Sources. I. Baron, Robert C. II. Title.
E302.A262 2009
973.4'4092--dc22
                          2009011510

Printed on recycled paper in Canada by Friesens Corp.
0 9 8 7 6 5 4 3 2 1

Design by Margaret McCullough
Cover image: *John Adams.* Pastel on paper by Benjamin Blyth, circa 1766. Massachusetts Historical Society.

Fulcrum Publishing
4690 Table Mountain Dr., Ste. 100
Golden, CO 80403
800-992-2908 • 303-277-1623
www.fulcrumbooks.com

CONTENTS

The Legacy of John Adams: Robert C. Baron............................ ix

An "Extravagant Passion": Beth Prindle................................. xv

The Adams Family Papers: C. James Taylor............................ xix

JOHN ADAMS, IN HIS OWN WORDS................................. 1

Adams on:
      AMERICA.. 11
      INDEPENDENCE.. 23
      GOVERNMENT.. 37
      FARMING.. 51
      SCIENCE AND TECHNOLOGY............................... 57
      EDUCATION... 61
      BOOKS AND LIBRARIES...................................... 67
      RELIGION AND RELIGIOUS FREEDOM............... 71
      FRIENDS AND FAMILY....................................... 77

Retirement and Correspondence with Thomas Jefferson......... 85

Acknowledgments.. 95

List of Correspondents... 96

Bibliography.. 100

THE LEGACY OF
JOHN ADAMS

*I will say for Mr. Adams, that he supported the Declaration with zeal
and ability, fighting fearlessly for every word of it.*

—*Thomas Jefferson*

JOHN ADAMS WAS BORN ON OCTOBER 30, 1735, in North
Braintree (now Quincy), Massachusetts, with his ancestry tracing
back to the earliest settlers of the Massachusetts Commonwealth.
His great-great grandparents, Henry and Edith Adams, had settled in
the small colony of Mount Wollaston (which later became Braintree)
in 1633, just four years after the creation of the Massachusetts Bay
Colony. Through his grandmother, he was a descendent of John
Alden, a Pilgrim who arrived on the *Mayflower*. His father, John
Adams, was a farmer, town selectman, and Congregational dea-
con, and his mother, Susannah Boylston, was a prominent early-
American socialite.

John, the eldest son, grew up in a community of books, ideas,
and deep conversation, passions that would shape his entire life.
He graduated from Harvard College in 1755. Although his father
wanted him to enter the ministry, he went to Worcester, a sixty-mile
horseback ride from his home, to teach school and think about his
career path. He soon chose the law for his profession and studied
under James Putnam, a successful lawyer in Worcester. Adams was
admitted to the bar in 1758 in Suffolk County.

Physically, Adams was a solid, stocky man, about five feet seven
inches tall, with blue eyes and a ruddy complexion. In 1764, at the
age of twenty-nine, he married Abigail Smith, nine years his junior
and the daughter of a minister, the Reverend William Smith of

Weymouth, Massachusetts. She was intelligent, well-read, and possessed strength of character and excellent interpersonal skills, characteristics readily apparent in the many letters that she sent Adams throughout their life together. The couple had six children and were married for almost fifty-four years, during which time their family moved between Braintree and Boston because of the demands of Adams's law practice. During this period, lawyers and judges would travel by horseback across various jurisdictions to hear and adjudicate cases, which resulted in Adams's frequent absences.

The prior half-century had been a good one for the colonies. The population had risen from 360,000 in 1713 to 1.6 million in 1763. Towns and colonies governed themselves with little interference from London, and there was loyalty to Great Britain and liberty under the law. Following the French and Indian War, however, the British government began to assert its power more aggressively and passed laws that directly, and often adversely, affected the colonies. The situation became tense, and in 1770 a street confrontation resulted in the death of five civilians, an event that would be referred to as the Boston Massacre. Adams successfully served as counsel for the British soldiers, defending them from criminal charges because he believed that according to the law, everyone was entitled to legal representation. Despite his support of the British soldiers, Adams was an early critic of Great Britain's policies—although not to the level of his firebrand cousin Sam Adams—and he opposed the Stamp Act of 1765 in writing and in person.

Adams was elected to the Colonial Legislature in June 1770 and became a delegate to the First Continental Congress in 1774 and the Second Continental Congress from 1775 until 1778. He was a driving force behind the push for independence, proposing George Washington as commander in chief of the Continental Army and resigning his seat on the Massachusetts Superior Court to become head of the Board of War and Ordnance for the Continental Congress. He served on many other committees, including the one appointed to write the Declaration of Independence. Though Jefferson is credited for drafting most of the document, Adams served a major role in the defense and promotion of the document in the ensuing debates on its adoption.

Around this same time, Adams worked on another committee, alongside Benjamin Franklin and three others, to write the Model Treaty, which provided the template for treaties by the Continental Congress, outlining free trade with all nations but permanent alliances with none. This document is now known as America's first diplomatic statement.

Adams represented the Continental Congress in Europe first in April 1778 through June 1779 and again starting in the fall of 1779, both in France and in the Netherlands. He served as the ambassador to the Netherlands from 1782 to 1788 and obtained several loans from Amsterdam that enabled the colonies to continue the Revolutionary War and pay for the peace. Adams was a major negotiator of the peace treaty with Great Britain, signing the treaty in September 1783. He became the first ambassador to Great Britain in 1785 and negotiated a peace treaty with Prussia the same year.

With the new Constitution in place, the question arose of who would become the first president. George Washington was elected unanimously to two terms. Adams, with the second most votes, became vice president from April 1789 to March 1797. When Washington retired, the 1796 presidential campaign became the first contested election in US history. Adams won by a slim margin, with 71 electoral votes, and Thomas Jefferson, with 68 votes, became vice president.

Adams served as president from March 1797 to March 1801. As is clear in his writings, these were not always the happiest years of Adams's life, partly due to the chaos in the nation's developing new capital. During his presidency, Adams broke with Alexander Hamilton and other Federalists in order to avoid war with France and thereby lost the support of the Federalist Party, making the political situation tense at home as well as abroad. In the election of 1800, one of the most hard-fought and bitter campaigns in US history, Adams lost to Jefferson and retired to his farm, Peacefield, near Quincy. While their relationship had been tested, Adams and Jefferson rekindled their friendship after Jefferson's departure from office in 1809, continuing a correspondence that is one of the most significant set of letters in US history.

In addition to his service as a diplomat and executive, Adams also had major influence as a writer. Many selections from those works are included in this book and in the volumes listed in the bibliography. In 1765 Adams wrote four articles for the *Boston Gazette* that were later published in 1768 in London as *A Dissertation on the Canon and the Feudal Law*. In 1772 he wrote *Novanglus; or, A History of the Dispute with America, from Its Origin in 1754 to the Present Time, 1774*. His 1776 book, *Thoughts on Government*, influenced many state constitutions as well as the Federal Constitution, and Adams himself penned the majority of the Massachusetts Constitution, the oldest constitution in the world. In 1787 he wrote *A Defence of the Constitutions of Government of the United States of America*, which was published in London. After leaving the presidency, Adams started his autobiography, which covers a part of his life and the world he witnessed.

John Adams died on July 4, 1826, the fiftieth anniversary of the Declaration of Independence, and only a few hours after the death of Thomas Jefferson. Adams always doubted his place in history, once saying, "Mausoleums, statues, monuments will never be erected to me." He questioned himself in his journals and his autobiography. He fought with authors such as John Taylor and Mercy Warren, whom he thought had not gotten history right. The marginalia in the books in his library show a man who loved controversy and wanted even his books to reflect and be marked by his thoughts. He was always pushing himself, continually studying, documenting events and his impressions of others. This is evidenced by his journals and in his letters to his wife, Abigail, and to Jefferson and others. Throughout the course of his twenty-five-year retirement, he continued to read, write, and argue about a variety of subjects.

A voice of the Revolution, a diplomat in Europe during the United States' formative years, a strong influence on the Declaration of Independence and the Constitution, a vice president and president who kept the country out of European wars, a farmer, author, and reader, John Adams was a man full of life. In a letter to Thomas Jefferson seven months before they both died, he wrote of a meeting with Jefferson's granddaughter Ellen Randolph Coolidge: "She said she had heard you say that you would like to go over life again. In this I could not agree; I would rather go forward and meet whatever is to come."

John and Abigail's descendents have had great influence on this country and are even referred to as the Adams political family. Their son John Quincy Adams became our sixth president. Their grandson Charles Francis Adams Sr. was a congressman who used his position as minister to Great Britain to ensure Britain's neutrality during the Civil War. Their great-grandson Henry Brooks Adams was a historian and noted author.

There are no indispensable people in history. But three who can almost claim that honor in the founding of this country are the first three presidents, George Washington, John Adams, and Thomas Jefferson—in essence the sword, the mind, and the heart of the United States' formative years. As the mind, Adams was a man who loved to debate, whether it be by speaking or by writing letters or essays. Thus, we are blessed with a wealth of his words to give us a window into that mind. This volume contains a selection of both his professional and personal writings, a wide range that gives insight into a powerful personality, an important mind, and a patriotic passion.

—*Robert C. Baron*

An "Extravagant" Passion
John Adams and His Library

I am mostly intent at present upon collecting a library, and I find that a great deal of thought and care, as well as money, are necessary to assemble an ample and well chosen assortment of books.

But when this is done, it is only a means, an instrument. Whenever I shall have completed my library, my end will not be answered. Fame, fortune, power say some, are the ends intended by a library. The service of God, country, clients, fellow men, say others. Which of these lie nearest my heart?

—*Diary of John Adams*
January 30, 1768

John Adams's library is special, not only because it has remained intact to the present day or because it constitutes one of the largest personal libraries collected in the United States during the second president's lifetime. This original collection of more than 3,500 books is most remarkable because it provides firsthand insight into how John Adams's lifelong dedication to reading and books shaped not only his personal history but US history as well.

Adams set forth quite deliberately to educate himself by collecting books on an immense variety of subjects and by engaging the great thinkers, philosophers, and political minds through their writings. His lifelong engagement was active and argumentative, as evidenced by the meticulous and voluminous personal commentary he crowded into the margins of many works he read. In those annotated volumes, one encounters an intimate and candid conversation with the wider world of "self culture through books" that engaged

Adams at every stage of his long life—as a young boy, university student, Boston lawyer, revolutionary, Founding Father, diplomat, president, and citizen of the early American republic.

From an early age, John Adams devoted a significant portion of his income to purchasing books. In 1771, at the age of thirty-six, the young Massachusetts lawyer resolved to make a steady investment in books. As Adams wrote to nephew Isaac Smith in London, "I want to agree with some Bookseller of character in whom I could entirely confide to send me Books whenever I shall want them and write for them as long as I shall live. As I am a little inclined to be extravagant in that kind of Entertainment, it is very likely I may write for Books to the amount of twenty, perhaps thirty, Pounds sterling a year." Adams could not resist the temptation presented by books and spent impressive sums on them, however meager his income. Although Adams's book collecting was primarily utilitarian, many of the books he acquired were quite rare, even in his own day. Adams claimed that he had spent "a fortune on books," and many volumes today prove the value, financial as well as intellectual, of Adams's significant investment.

Among the extant volumes in John Adams's library are hundreds of books acquired during his embassies to France, Holland, and England, including books known to have been used in the drafting of his influential *A Defence of the Constitutions of Government of the United States of America* in 1787. Adams's law books, collected largely during the 1760s, include half a dozen annotated volumes whose contents were explicitly employed in his successful defense of the British troops indicted after the Boston Massacre. His copy of William Gordon's eyewitness *The History of the Rise, Progress, and Establishment, of the Independence of the United States of America* (London, 1788) is peppered with Adams's bitter manuscript notes, angrily revising Gordon's contemporary interpretation of Adams's role in the American Revolution and the elevation of other founders' reputations over his own. In these annotated pages of his personal library, Adams is a tangibly felt presence, along with his wife, Abigail, his eldest son, John Quincy Adams, and the rivals, friends, and partners of a complicated political lifetime, including Thomas Jefferson, Alexander Hamilton, George Washington, and John Marshall.

To read Adams's marginal notations is to listen in on his conversations with writers across oceans and across centuries, as he mentally enters a timeless world in which all the writers exist and speak in a simultaneous present. For example, in 1770, as Adams prepared to defend the British soldiers on trial after the Boston Massacre, he referenced ancient Roman advocate Marcus Tullius Cicero's similar view on self-defense in the margins of contemporary British jurist William Blackstone's *Commentaries on the Laws of England*. While the printed text of his books remained static, John Adams's scribbled reactions were in constant process. He reread his books—and his own comments—at various times in his life, and, by dating his new notes and self-critiques, he offers a window into who he was at that time and what was transpiring in the world around him. Through this self-education, Adams honed his own philosophies, synthesizing the best of what had come before him, critically observing the work of his contemporaries, and refining both in the context of the American revolutionary experiment. His dynamic, addictive reading gave force to his shaping of key documents of American government and civil liberties and responsibilities.

John Adams's handwritten marginal commentaries span his lifetime and his library, exhibiting his experiences in all the dimensions of youth, maturity, and age. He voraciously absorbed all he could from his books, turned his formed opinions into the heat of revolutionary and diplomatic action, and then, in retirement, reflected on his life and his reading. Not only are volumes extensively annotated in Adams's own hand, but they are often the repository of other objects, such as letters, notes, and the autumnal pressed leaves of familiar New England trees. Adams's first book, a small copy of Cicero's *Orations*, is decorated with smudges, pen trails, and a swaggeringly grandiose signature; it shows the tattered wear of being jammed into the pocket of the fourteen-year-old youth Adams was when he received it. His personal copy of Thomas Paine's *Common Sense*, one of the most influential pamphlets of the Revolutionary War era, was purchased in 1776 during Adams's ride on horseback from his farm in Massachusetts to the Second Continental Congress, in Philadelphia. Adams's copy of *Common Sense* is poignantly travel-worn, its pages dog-eared and stained with food and drink. He was so impressed with its content that he bought a second copy to send home to his wife, Abigail.

Amassing the library, even reading every title on its shelves, was not the goal for John Adams. As the thirty-two-year-old Adams penned in his diary in 1768, the library was "only a means, an instrument." "Whenever I shall have completed my library, my end will not be answered," he wrote. He mused that the acquisition of "Fame, fortune, power" might be "the ends intended by a library." On the other hand, the ends might be "service" to "God, country, clients, fellow men." Shaped by the experience of the books, the reader was to seek action in the world. Thus, when Adams completed his library in the final years of his life, his larger end was not answered. He wanted his books, annotations and all, to be placed into the service of his country and fellow men. By the 1822 donation of his library to a school in his native Quincy, Massachusetts, and its subsequent transfer to the Boston Public Library in 1894, Adams left a fitting monument for a man so devoted to books and learning. John Adams's extravagant passion for books has become a public treasure: the property of the people and free to all.

—Beth Prindle
Manager, John Adams Library
Boston Public Library

THE ADAMS FAMILY PAPERS

The Adams Family Papers at the Massachusetts Historical Society (MHS) is a unique collection of manuscripts documenting the lives of this prominent American family and the public events in which they participated. The work of several generations of thoughtful and articulate Adams men and women, the collection contains over 300,000 pages of diaries, autobiographies, correspondence, and other writings. It is a peerless source for any study of the period from about 1750 to 1900.

The founding generation's John Adams set the standard, urging his wife, Abigail, to write and to encourage their children to write. He advised that "the Faculty of Writing is attainable, by Art, Practice, and Habit only. The sooner, therefore the Practice begins, the more likely it will be to succeed." The Adams family's penchant for putting pen to paper originated as an obligation to a demanding father but became a service to posterity.

John Adams emerged as a staunch advocate for the written record during his tenure in the Continental Congress when he realized that his correspondence, diary, and other writings would live on to help chronicle the nation's founding. In June 1776 he lamented to Abigail that "during a Course of twenty Years at least that I have been a Writer of Letters I never kept a Single Copy." (Fortunately, Abigail and others had.) To correct this deficiency, John purchased a blank book in which he copied his letters. He continued this practice throughout his public life, preserving a record of letters that subsequently went astray.

The papers amassed by John and Abigail Adams by the end of the eighteenth century came to rest at the family residence in Quincy, Massachusetts—the "Old House"—and remained there, augmented by each new generation, until the turn of the next century. After 1870 a specially constructed Stone Library housed the collection.

In 1902 the papers were transferred to the recently erected Boylston Street building of the MHS. The family retained ownership and strict control under the Adams Manuscript Trust, created in 1906 to protect the papers from the public glare. Over the next fifty years access was closed to all but a chosen few. Given the outspokenness of the Adamses, the family feared that unregulated use of the papers could invite ridicule of their forebears or embarrass their friends and even their opponents.

The passage of time eroded the concern of the Adamses about open access to the family papers. In 1956 they transferred ownership to the MHS. The modern editions of the Franklin and Jefferson papers had been launched by this time, and the Adamses desired that their family's papers be given the same scholarly treatment. The society responded by establishing an editorial project dedicated to the publication of the papers. Now, over fifty years and more than forty volumes later, the Adams Family Papers, with a third generation of editors, continues to provide scholars and an interested public with the best possible access to the collection. The full archive is available at institutions throughout the United States and beyond in the form of a 608-reel microfilm copy. Significant parts of the collection can also be found online at the MHS website, www.masshist.org. John Adams's diary and autobiography, his correspondence with Abigail, and John Quincy Adams's diary appear either as manuscript page images or as manuscript and printed text. All of the printed volumes prepared by the editors through 2006 have been digitized for the website. This documentary treasure held so closely by the Adams family for generations is now freely accessible throughout the world.

—C. James Taylor
Editor in Chief, The Adams Family Papers
Massachusetts Historical Society

JOHN ADAMS, IN HIS OWN WORDS

John Adams kept a diary throughout much of his early life and wrote parts of an autobiography after he had left the presidency. In his writing he was candid and forthcoming, honestly revealing his thoughts and feelings to friends and rivals alike. During his long absences from home, as a lawyer on the Massachusetts circuit, in Philadelphia, New York, and Europe, he wrote and received almost 300 letters from his "dearest friend," Abigail. The letters were witty and serious, dealing with affairs of the country and the family, providing information, opinions, and concerns. Their correspondence from 1762 to 1801 shows a couple ardently committed to one another and deeply in love, in spite of the distance that frequently separated them.

NO MAN IS ENTIRELY FREE FROM WEAKNESS and imperfection in this life. Men of the most exalted genius and active minds are generally most perfect slaves to the love of fame. They sometimes descend to as mean tricks and artifices in pursuit of honor or reputation as the miser descends to in pursuit of gold.

—*Diary of John Adams*
February 19, 1756

THE LOVE OF FAME NATURALLY BETRAYS A MAN into several weaknesses and fopperies that tend very much to diminish his reputation, and so defeat itself.

—*Diary of John Adams*
May 3, 1756

NATURE AND TRUTH, or rather truth and right are invariably the same in all times and in all places; and reason, pure unbiased reason, perceives them alike in all times and in all places.

—*Diary of John Adams*
May 11, 1756

WHAT IS THE PROPER BUSINESS OF MANKIND in this life? We come into the world naked, and destitute of all the conveniences and necessaries of life; and if we were not provided for and nourished by our parents, or others, should inevitably perish as soon as born; we increase in strength of body and mind, by slow and insensible degrees; one third of our time is consumed in sleep, and three sevenths of the remainder is spent in procuring a mere animal sustenance; and if we live to the age of threescore and ten, and then sit down to make an estimate in our minds of the happiness we have enjoyed, and the misery we have suffered, we shall find, I am apt to think, that the overbalance of happiness is quite inconsiderable.

—*Diary of John Adams*
May 29, 1756

HE IS NOT A WISE MAN, and is unfit to fill any important station in society, that has left one passion in his soul unsubdued.

—*Diary of John Adams*
June 14, 1756

I AM RESOLVED TO RISE WITH THE SUN... May I blush whenever I suffer one hour to pass unimproved. I will rouse up my mind and fix my attention; I will stand collected within myself and think upon what I read and what I see. I will strive with all my soul to be something more than persons who have had less advantages than myself.

—Diary of John Adams
July 21, 1756

HOW IT IS WITH YOU I KNOW NOT, but I am rightly informed, I am yet alive and not dead. And to prove it to you, I will tell you how I live. I Sleep 12 or 13 Hours, Smoke 10 or 12 Pipes, read 5 or 6 Pages, Think 19 or 20 Ideas, and eat 3 or 4 meals every 24 hours. I have either mounted above or sunk below. I have not Penetration enough to say which, all Thoughts of Fame, Fortune, or even Matrimony.

—Letter to William Crawford
October 1758

TAKE MY ADVICE; rise and mount your horse by the morning's dawn, and shake away, amidst the great and beautiful scenes of nature that appear at that time of the day, all the crudities that are left in your stomach, and all the obstructions that are left in your brains. Then return to your studies, and bend your whole soul to the institutes of the law and the cases that have adjudged by the rules of the institutes; let no trifling diversion, or amusement, or company, decoy you from your book; that is let no girl, or gun, no cards, no flutes, no violins, no dress, no tabacco, no laziness, decoy you from your books.

—Diary of John Adams
January 3, 1759

WHAT AM I DOING? Shall I sleep away my whole seventy years. No, by every thing I swear I will renounce the contemplative, and betake myself to an active, roving life by sea or land, or else. I will attempt some uncommon unexpected enterprize in law. Let me lay the plan and arouse spirit enough to push boldly.

—*Diary of John Adams*
January 3, 1759

NOW LET ME COLLECT MY THOUGHTS...Now let me form the great habits of thinking, writing, speaking...Let love and vanity be extinguished, and the great passions of ambition, patriotism, break out and burn. Let little objects be neglected and forgot, and great ones engross, arouse and exalt my soul. The mind must be aroused or it will slumber.

—*Diary of John Adams*
April 18, 1759

A PEN IS CERTAINLY AN EXCELLENT INSTRUMENT, to fix a Man's attention and to inflame his ambition.

—*Diary of John Adams*
November 14, 1760

LET US BELIEVE NO MAN TO BE INFALLIBLE or impeccable in government, any more than in religion.

—*From the* Boston Gazette *essay* "On Self-Delusion"
1763

THE DAY OF THE MONTH REMINDS ME of my birthday, which will be on the 30th. I was born Octr. 19, 1735 [Julian calendar]. Thirty Seven Years, more than half the Life of Man, are run out. What an atom, an animalcule I am! The remainder of my days I shall rather decline, in sense, spirit, and activity. My season for acquiring knowledge is past. And Yet I have my own and my children's fortunes to make. My boyish habits, and airs are not yet worn off.

—*Diary of John Adams*
October 19, 1772

MY LIFE HAS BEEN a continual Scene of Fatigue, Vexation, Labour and Anxiety. I have four Children. I had a pretty Estate from my Father, I have been assisted by your Father. I have done the greatest Business in the Province. I have had the very richest Clients in the Province: Yet I am Poor in Comparison of others.

—*Diary of John Adams*
June 29, 1774

AMONG ALL THE DISAPPOINTMENTS, and Perplexities, which have fallen to my share in Life, nothing has contributed so much to support my Mind, as the choice Blessing of a Wife, whose Capacity, enabled her to comprehend, and whose pure Virtue obliged her to approve the Views of her Husband. This has been the cheering Consolation of my Heart, in my most solitary gloomy and disconsolate Hours.

—*Letter to Abigail Adams*
May 22, 1776

I HAVE A VERY TENDER FEELING HEART. This Country knows not, and never can know the Torments, I have endured for its sake. I am glad they never can know, for it would give more Pain to the benevolent and humane, than I could wish, even the wicked and malicious to feel.

—Letter to Abigail Adams
August 18, 1776

TO TELL YOU THE TRUTH, I admire the Ladies here. Dont be jealous. They are handsome, and very well educated. Their Accomplishments are exceedingly brilliant. And their Knowledge of Letters and Arts, exceeds that of the English Ladies much, I believe.

—Letter to Abigail Adams
April 25, 1778

IF VIRTUE WAS TO BE REWARDED WITH WEALTH, it would not be Virtue. If Virtue was to be rewarded with Fame, it would not be Virtue of the sublimest Kind.

—Letter to Abigail Adams
December 2, 1778

VIRTUE IS NOT ALWAYS AMIABLE.

—Diary of John Adams
February 9, 1779

THERE IS A FEEBLENESS AND LANGUOR IN MY NATURE. My mind and body both partake of this weakness. By my physical constitution I am but an ordinary man. The times alone have destined me to fame; and even these have not been able to give me much. When I look into the glass, my eye, my forehead, my brow, my cheeks, my lips, all betray this relaxation. Yet when some great events, some cutting expressions, some mean hypocrisies, have, at times, thrown this assemblage of sloth, sleep, and littleness into a rage a little like a lion.

—Diary of John Adams
April 26, 1779

MY CHILDREN WILL NOT BE SO WELL LEFT by their father as he was by his. They will be infected with the Examples and Habits and Tastes for Expensive Living, without the means. He was not.

—Letter to Abigail Adams
December 2, 1781

AN HONEST, SENSIBLE HUMANE MAN, above all the Littlenesses of Vanity, and Extravagances of Imagination, labouring to do good rather than be rich to be usefull rather than make a show, living in a modest Simplicity clearly within his Means and free from Debts or Obligations, is really the most respectable Man in Society, makes himself and all about him the most happy.

—Letter to Abigail Adams
June 9, 1783

You know your Man. He will never be a Slave. He will never cringe. He will never accommodate his Principles, sentiments or Systems, to keep a Place, or to get a Place, no nor to please his Daughter, or his Wife. He will never depart from his Honour, his Duty, nor his honest Pride for Coaches, Tables, Gold, Power or Glory.

—*Letter to Abigail Adams*
July 17, 1783

Your letter of the 23d has made me the happiest Man upon Earth. I am twenty Years younger than I was Yesterday.

—*Letter to Abigail Adams*
July 26, 1784

There is none among them more essential or remarkable, than the *passion for distinction*. A desire to be observed, considered, esteemed, praised, beloved, and admired by his fellows, is one of the earliest, as well as keenest dispositions discovered in the heart of man.

—Discourses on Davila
April 1790–April 1791

Emulation, which is imitation and something more— a desire not only to equal or resemble, but to excel, is so natural a movement of the human heart, that, wherever men are to be found, and in whatever manner associated or connected, we see its effects.

—Discourses on Davila
April 1790–April 1791

THIS JOURNAL IS COMMENCED TO ALLURE ME into the habit of writing again, long lost. The habit is easily lost, but not easily regained. I have in the course of my life, lost it several times and regained it as often; so I will now.

—Diary of John Adams
July 12, 1796

OF ALL THE SUMMERS OF MY LIFE, this has been the freest from care, anxiety, and vexation to me, the sickness of Mrs. A. excepted. My health has been better, the seasons fruitful, my farm was well conducted. Alas! What may happen to reverse all this? But it is folly to anticipate evils, and madness to create imaginary ones.

—Diary of John Adams
August 4, 1796

WHAT MUST I SAY OF MY OWN VANITY AND LEVITY? Crimes, I thank God, I have none to report. Follies, indiscretions, and trifles, enough and too many.

—Letter to Benjamin Rush
July 23, 1806

NOW, SIR, TO BE SERIOUS, I do not curse the day when I engaged in public affairs. I do not say when I became a politician, for that I never was. I cannot repent of anything I ever did conscientiously and from a sense of duty. I never engaged in public offices for my own interest, pleasure, envy, jealously, avarice or ambition or even the desire for fame.

—Letter to Benjamin Rush
May 1, 1807

A MAN NEVER LOOKS SO SILLY as when he is talking or writing concerning himself.

—*Letter to Mercy Otis Warren*
July 27, 1807

MAUSOLEUMS, STATUES, MONUMENTS will never be erected to me. I wish them not. Panegyrical romances will never be written, nor flattering orations spoken, to transmit me to posterity in brilliant colors. No, nor in true colors. All but the last I loathe.

—*Letter to Benjamin Rush*
March 23, 1809

I AM LEFT ALONE. While Paine, Gerry and Lovell lived, there were some that I seemed to know, but now, not one of my contemporaries and colleagues is left. Can there be any deeper damnation in the universe, than to be condemned to a long life, in danger, toil, and anxiety.

—*Letter to Rufous King*
December 2, 1814

I HAVE AS GREAT A TERROR OF LEARNED LADIES, as you have. I have such a consciousness of Inferiority to them, as mortifies and humiliates my self-love, to such a degree that I can scarcely speak in their presence. Very few of these Ladies have ever had the condenscation to allow me to talk. And when it has so happened, I have always come off mortified at the discovery of my Inferiority.

—*Letter to François Adriaan van der Kemp*
April 8, 1815

ADAMS ON AMERICA

America, to John Adams, was a special place. For 140 years, from 1620 to 1760, the colonies and their inhabitants possessed the same freedoms and responsibilities of all British people. They had local government, taxation with the consent of the citizens, and a legal system that had been established starting with the Magna Carta. When their freedoms were challenged and it became impossible to resolve issues peacefully with Britain, Adams was a leader in the fight for independence. His time spent in France, Holland, and England revealed to him more clearly than ever the special nature of the United States, which he documented in his extensive writings. To John Adams, the United States was the future of all mankind.

CONSIDER FOR ONE MINUTE THE CHANGES produced in this country within the space of two hundred years. Then the whole continent was one continued dismal wilderness, the haunt of wolves and bears and more savage men. Now the forests are removed, the land covered with fields of corn, orchards bending with fruit, and the magnificent habitations of rational and civilized people. Then, our rivers flowed through gloomy deserts and offensive swamps. Now, the same rivers glide smoothly on, through rich countries fraught with every delightful object, and through meadows painted with the most beautiful scenery of nature and art.

—Diary of John Adams
June 14, 1756

WHO CAN STUDY IN BOSTON STREETS? I am unable to observe the various Objects that I meet, with sufficient Precision. My Eyes are so diverted with Chimney Sweepers, Carriers of Wood, Merchants, Ladies, Priests, Carts, Horses, Oxen, Coaches, Market men and women, Soldiers, Sailors; and my Ears with the Rattle-Gabble of them all that I cannot think long enough in the Street upon any one thing, to start and pursue a Thought. I cannot raise my mind above the mob Crowd of Men, Women, Beasts and Carriages to think steadily.

—*Diary of John Adams*
March 18, 1759

NOW TO WHAT HIGHER OBJECT, to what greater character, can any mortal aspire than to be possessed of all this knowledge, well digested and ready at command, to assist the feeble and friendless, to discountenance the haughty and lawless, to procure redress of wrongs, the advancement of right, to assert and maintain liberty and virtue, to discourage and abolish tyranny and vice?

—*Letter to Jonathan Sewall*
October 1759

I ALWAYS CONSIDER the settlement of America with reverence and wonder, as the opening of a grand scene and design in providence, for the illumination of the ignorant and the emancipation of the slavish part of mankind all over the earth.

—*Diary of John Adams*
February 1765

NO ONE OF ANY FEELING, born and educated in this once happy country, can consider the numerous distresses, the gross indignities, the barbarous ignorance, the haughty usurpations, that we have reason to fear are mediating for ourselves, our children, our neighbors, in short, for all our countrymen and all their posterity, without the utmost agonies of heart and many tears.

—A Dissertation on the Canon and the Feudal Law
1765

A MILITIA LAW, REQUIRING ALL MEN, or with very few exceptions besides cases of conscience, to be provided with arms and ammunition, to be trained at certain seasons; and requiring counties, towns, or other small districts, to be provided with public stocks of ammunition and intrenching utensils, and with some settled plans for transporting provisions after the militia, when marched to defend their country against sudden invasions, and requiring certain districts to be provided with field-pieces, companies of matrosses, and perhaps some regiments of light-horse, is always a wise institution, and, in the present circumstances of our country, indispensable.

—Thoughts on Government
March–April 1776

A CONSTITUTION FOUNDED ON THESE PRINCIPLES introduces knowledge among the people, and inspires them with a conscious dignity becoming freemen; a general emulation takes place, which causes good humor, sociability, good manners, and good morals to be general.

—Thoughts on Government
March–April 1776

I AM SURPRIZED AT THE SUDDENNESS, as well as Greatness of this Revolution...It is the will of Heaven, that the two countries should be sundered forever. It may be the will of Heaven that America shall suffer, Calamities still more wasting and Distresses yet more dreadfull. If this is to be the Case it will have this good Effect, at least: it will inspire Us with many Virtues which We have not, and correct many Errors, Follies, and Vices which threaten to disturb, dishonor, and destroy us. The Furnace of Affliction produces Refinement, in states as well as Individuals. And the new Governments we are assuming, in every Part, will require a Purification from our Vices, and an Augmentation of our Virtues, or they will be no Blessings. The People will have unbounded Power. And the People are extreamly addicted to Corruption and Venality, as well as the Great. I am not without apprehension from this quarter. But I must submit, all my Hopes and Fears to an overruling Providence, in which, unfashionable as the Faith may be, I firmly believe.

—*Letter to Abigail Adams*
July 3, 1776

I FEEL AN INCLINATION SOMETIMES, to write the History of the last Three Years, in Imitation of Thucidides. There is a striking Resemblance, in several Particulars, between the Peloponnesian and the American War. The real Motive to the former was a Jealousy of the growing Power of Athens, by Sea and Land. The genuine Motive to the latter, was a similar Jealousy of the growing Power of America. The true Causes which incite to War, are seldom, professed, or Acknowledged.

—*Letter to Abigail Adams*
August 20, 1777

THIS EVENING HAD A LITTLE CONVERSATION with the Chevalier upon our American affairs and characters,—Mr. Samuel Adams, Mr. Dickinson, Mr. Jay,—and upon American eloquence in Congress and assemblies, as well as in writing. He admired our eloquence. I said that our eloquence was not corrected. It was the time of Ennius with us. That Mr. Dickinson and Mr. Jay had eloquence; but it was not so chaste, nor pure, nor nervous, as that of Mr. Samuel Adams. That this last had written some things that would be admired more than any thing that has been written in America in the dispute.

—Diary of John Adams
June 20, 1778

I WAS NEVER MORE AMUSED with political speculations, than since my arrival in this country. Every one has his prophecy, and every prophecy is a paradox. One says, America will give France the go-by. Another, that France and Spain will abandon America. A third, that Spain will forsake France and America. A fourth, that America has the interest of all Europe against her. A fifth, that she will become the greatest manufacturing country, and thus ruin Europe, A sixth, that she will become a great military and naval power, and will be very ambitious, and so terrible to Europe. In short, it seems as if they had studied for every impossibility, and great to foretell it, as a possible future event.

—Letter to Benjamin Franklin
August 17, 1780

FOR MY OWN PART, I thought America had been long enough involved in the wars of Europe. She had been a foot-ball between contending nations from the beginning, and it was easy to foresee that France and England both would endeavor to involve us in their future wars. I thought it our interest and duty to avoid as much as possible, and to be completely independent, and have nothing to do, but in commerce, with either of them.

—Diary of John Adams
October 11, 1782

IT HAS BEEN THE GENERAL SENSE OF OUR COUNTRY, since the peace, that it was their duty and their interest to be impartial between the powers of Europe, and observe a neutrality in their wars. This principle is a wise one, upon the supposition that these powers will be impartial to us, and permit us to remain at peace.

—Letter to John Jay
October 17, 1785

I FIND I SHALL BE ACCABLÉ with Business and Ceremony together, and I miss my fine walks and pure Air at Auteuil. The Smoke and Damp of this City is ominous to me. London boasts of its Trottoir, but there is a space between it and the Houses through which all the Air from Kitchens, Cellars, Stables and Servants Appartements ascends into the Street and pours directly on the Passenger on Foot. Such Whiffs and puffs assault you every few Steps as are enough to breed the Plague if they do not Suffocate you on the Spot.

—Letter to Thomas Jefferson
June 7, 1785

THE ONLY PRACTICABLE METHOD, therefore, of giving to farmers, &c. the equal right of citizens, and then proper weight and influence in society, is by elections, frequently repeated, of a house of commons, an assembly which shall be an essential part of the sovereignty.

—A Defence of the Constitutions of the United States of America
1786–1787

THE LANGUAGES OF EUROPE are now becoming of such importance to us, and every gentleman employed under the United States, in the diplomatic department, ought to take all reasonable methods to acquaint himself with them.

—*Letter to William Smith*
April 11, 1787

THE SITUATION OF OUR COUNTRY is not like that of most of the nations in Europe. They have, generally, large numbers of inhabitants in narrow territories. We have small numbers scattered over vast regions.

—*Letter to President Washington*
August 29, 1790

As long as there is patriotism, there will be national emulation, vanity, and pride. It is national pride which commonly stimulates kings and ministers. National fear, apprehension of danger, and the necessity of self-defence, is added to such rivalries for wealth, consideration, and power. The safety, independence, and existence of a nation, depend upon keeping up a high sense of its own honor, dignity, and power, in the hearts of its individuals, and a lively jealousy of the growing power and aspiring ambition of a neighboring state.

—Discourses on Davila
April 1790–April 1791

Yesterday I dined at the President's, with ministers of state and their ladies, foreign and domestic. After dinner the gentlemen drew off after the ladies, and left me alone with the President in close conversation. He detained me there till nine o'clock, and was never more frank and open upon politics. I find his opinions and sentiments are more exactly like mine than I ever knew before, respecting England, France, and our American parties.

—*Diary of John Adams*
March 25, 1796

My dearest Friend, your dearest Friend never had a more trying day than Yesterday. A Solemn Scene it was indeed and it was made more affecting to me, by the Presence of the General, whose Countenance was as serene and unclouded as the day. He Seem'd to me to enjoy a Tryumph over me. Methought I heard him think Ay! I am fairly out and you fairly in! See which of Us will be happiest.

—*Letter to Abigail Adams*
March 5, 1797

LAST NIGHT FOR THE FIRST TIME I slept in our new House. But what a Scene! The Furniture belonging to the Publick is in the most deplorable Condition. There is not a Chair fit to sit in. The Beds and Bedding are in a woeful Pickle. This House has been a scene of the most scandalous Drinkenness and Disorder among the servants, that ever I heard of.

—Letter to Abigail Adams
March 22, 1797

I WILL NEVER SEND ANOTHER MINISTER TO FRANCE, without assurances that he will be received, respected, and honored as the representative of a great, free, powerful, and independent nation.

—Message to Congress
June 21, 1798

I LIKE THE SEAT OF GOVERNMENT VERY WELL and shall Sleep, or lie awake next Winter in the Presidents house. I have Slept very well on my Journey and been pretty well.

—Letter to Abigail Adams
June 13, 1800

WHY SHOULD WE TAKE the bread out of the mouths of our own children and give it to strangers? We do so much of this in the army, navy, and especially in the consulship abroad, that it frequently gives me great anxiety.

—Letter to John Marshall
August 14, 1800

I PRAY HEAVEN TO BESTOW THE BEST OF BLESSINGS on this House [the White House] and all that shall hereafter inhabit it. May none but honest and wise Men ever rule under this roof.

—Letter to Abigail Adams
November 2, 1800

I HEREBY AUTHORIZE AND REQUEST you to execute the office of Secretary of State so far as to affirm the seal of the United States to the inclosed commission to the present Secretary of State, John Marshall, of Virginia, to be chief justice of the United States.

—Letter to Samuel Dexter
January 31, 1801

I AM WILLING YOU should call this the Age of Frivolity as you do: and would not object if you had named it the Age of Folly, Vice, Frenzy, Fury, Brutality, Daemons, Buonaparte, Tom Paine, or the Age of the burning Brand from the bottomless Pitt; or any thing but the Age of Reason.

—Letter to Dr. Benjamin Waterhouse
October 29, 1805

I AM SUSPICIOUS, nay persuaded, they [Great Britain] have not only the impressed and enlisted American seamen on board their men-of-war to an amount of many thousands, but many more in the merchant ships and their transports.

—Letter to James Monroe
February 23, 1813

CAN YOU ACCOUNT for the apathy, the antipathy of this nation to their own history? Is there not a repugnance to the thought of looking back? While thousand of frivolous novels are read with eagerness and got by heart, the history of our own native country is not only neglected, but despised and abhorred.

—*Letter to Thomas McKean*
August 31, 1813

Adams on Independence

John Adams was a highly influential advocate for independence whose fierce dedication to the cause and unwavering personal ethics made him one of its most important supporters. He opposed the Stamp Act and wrote that the colonists shared the Englishman's right to be taxed only with their consent and to be tried by a jury of one's peers. He successfully defended the British soldiers charged with the Boston Massacre, believing that everyone had an equal right to legal representation under the law. His political essays were major contributions to the discussions in the colonies and in Britain. Adams was a delegate to the first and second Continental Congresses, and when war broke out in 1776, he was appointed president of the Board of War and Ordnance. Adams served on the committee to draft the Declaration of Independence and proposed that Thomas Jefferson write the document. In 1777 Adams was made a joint commissioner to France, raised loans for the war in the Netherlands, and helped negotiate the peace treaty with Britain. In 1785 he was made the first ambassador to Great Britain.

THE YEAR 1765 has been the most remarkable Year of my Life. That enormous Engine, fabricated by the British Parliament, for battering down all the Rights and Liberties of America, I mean the Stamp Act, has raised and spread, thro the whole Continent, a Spirit that will be recorded to our Honour, with all future Generations.

—*Diary of John Adams*
December 18, 1765

BE NOT INTIMIDATED, therefore, by any terrors, from publishing with the utmost freedom, whatever can be warranted by the laws of your country; nor suffer yourselves to be wheedled out of your liberty by any pretences of politeness, delicacy, or decency. These, as they are often used, are but three different names for hypocrisy, chicanery, and cowardice.

—A Dissertation on the Canon and the Feudal Law
1765

LET US RECOLLECT it was liberty, the hope of liberty for themselves and us and ours, which conquered all discouragements, dangers, and trials.

—A Dissertation on the Canon and the Feudal Law
1765

WE TAKE IT CLEARLY, THEREFORE, to be inconsistent with the spirit of the common law, and of the essential fundamental principles of the British constitution, that we should be subject to any tax imposed by the British Parliament; because we are not represented in that assembly in any sense, unless it be by a fiction of law, as insensible in theory as it would be injurious in practice, if such a taxation should be grounded on it.

—*Instructions of the town of Braintree
to their representative (Ebenezer Thayer)*
October 14, 1765

FACTS ARE STUBBORN THINGS; and whatever may be our wishes, our inclinations, or the dictates of our passions, they cannot alter the state of facts and evidence. Nor is the law less stable than the facts.

—*Argument in defense of the British soldiers in the Boston Massacre Trial*
December 4, 1770

THE DYE IS CAST: The People have passed the River and cutt away the Bridge: last Night Three Cargoes of Tea, were emptied into the Harbour. This is the grandest Event, which has ever yet happened Since, the Controversy, with Britain, opened!

—*Letter to James Warren*
December 17, 1773

LAST NIGHT, three cargoes of Bohea tea were emptied into the sea. This morning a man-of-war sails. This is the most magnificent movement of all. There is a dignity, a majesty, a sublimity, in this last effort of the patriots, that I greatly admire. The people should never rise without doing something to be remembered, something notable and striking. This destruction of the tea is so bold, so daring, so firm, intrepid and inflexible, and it must have so important consequences, and so lasting, that I cannot but consider it as an epocha in history.

—*Diary of John Adams*
December 17, 1773

WE LIVE MY DEAR SOUL, in an Age of Tryal. What will be the Consequence I know not. The Town of Boston, for ought I can See, must Suffer Martyrdom. It must expire. And our principal Consolation is, that it dies in a noble Cause. The Cause of Truth, of Virtue, of Liberty and of Humanity, and that it will probably have a glorious Reformation, to greater Wealth, Splendor and Power than ever.

—Letter to Abigail Adams
May 12, 1774

THERE IS LITTLE DANGER from any Thing We shall do, at the Congress. There is such a spirit, thro the Colonies, and the Members of Congress are such Characters, that no Danger can happen to Us, which will not involve the whole Continent, in Universal Desolation, and in that Case who would wish to live?

—Letter to Abigail Adams
September 8, 1774

IN A CAUSE WHICH INTERESTS the whole Globe, at a Time, when my Friends and Country, are in such keen Distress, I am scarcely ever interrupted, in the least Degree, by Apprehensions for my Person Safety.

—Letter to Abigail Adams
May 2, 1775

OUR PROSPECT OF A UNION OF THE COLONIES, is promising indeed. Never was there such a Spirit. Yet I feel anxious, because, there is always more Smoke than Fire—more Noise than Musick.

—Letter to Abigail Adams
May 8, 1775

I FIND THAT THE GENERAL SENSE ABROAD is to prepare for a vigorous defense War, but at the same time to keep open the door of reconciliation; to hold the Sword in one Hand and the Olive branch in the other.

—Letter to Moses Gill
June 10, 1775

WE ARE LOST in the extensiveness of our field of business. We have a continental treasury to establish, a paymaster to choose and a committee of correspondence or safety, of accounts, or something, I know not what, has confounded us all this day.

—Letter to James Warren
July 24, 1775

THIS YEAR BRINGS RUIN OR SALVATION to the British colonies. The eyes of all America is fixed on the [British] parliament. In short Britain and America are staring at each other, and they will probably stare more and more for some time.

—Diary of John Adams
January 1, 1776

THE EVENTS OF WAR ARE UNCERTAIN: We cannot insure Success, but We can deserve it.

—Letter to Abigail Adams
February 18, 1776

YOU AND I, MY DEAR FRIEND, have been sent into life at a time when the greatest lawgivers of antiquity would have wished to live. How few of the human race have ever enjoyed an opportunity of making an election of government, more than of air, soil or climate, for themselves or their children! When before the present epoch, have three millions of people full power and a fair opportunity to form and establish the wisest and happiest government that human wisdom can contrive?

—Thoughts on Government
March–April 1776

THE DONS, the bashers, the grandees, the patricians, the sachems, the nabobs, call them by what name you please, sigh, and groan, and fret, and sometimes stamp, and foam, and curse, but all in vain. The decree is gone forth, and it cannot be recalled, that a more equal liberty than has prevailed in other parts of the earth must be established in America.

—*Letter to Patrick Henry*
June 3, 1776

I THINK WITH YOU, that every colony should furnish its proportion of men, and I hope it will come to this. But at present some colonies have such bodies of Quakers, and Mennonites, and Moravians, who are principled against war, and others have such bodies as tories, or cowards, or unprincipled people who will not wage war; that it is, as yet, impossible.

—*Letter to Nathanael Greene*
June 22, 1776

YESTERDAY THE GREATEST QUESTION WAS DECIDED, which ever was debated in America, and a greater perhaps, never was or will be decided among Men. A Resolution was passed without one dissenting Colony "that these united Colonies, are, and of right ought to be free and independent States."

—Letter to Abigail Adams
July 3, 1776

BUT ON THE OTHER HAND, the Delay of this Declaration to this Time, has many great Advantages attending it.—The Hopes of Reconciliation, which were fondly entertained by Multitudes of honest and well meaning tho weak and mistaken People, have been gradually and at last totally extinguished.—Time has been given for the whole People, maturely to consider the great Question of Independence and to ripen their judgments, dissipate their Fears, and allure their Hopes, by discussing it in News Papers and Pamphletts, by debating it, in Assemblies, Conventions, Committees of Safety and Inspection, in Town and County Meetings, as well as in private Conversations, so that the whole People in every Colony of the 13, have now adopted it, as their own Act.—This will cement the Union, and avoid those Heats and perhaps Convulsions which might have been occasioned, by such a Declaration Six Months ago. But the Day is past. The Second Day of July 1776, will be the most memorable Epocha, in the History of America. I am apt to believe that it will be celebrated, by succeeding Generations, as the great anniversary Festival. It ought to be commemorated, as the Day of Deliverance by solemn Acts of Devotion to God Almighty. It ought to be solemnized with Pomp and Parade, with Shews, Games, Sports, Guns, Bells, Bonfires and Illuminations from one End of this Continent to the other from this Time forward forevermore.

—Second letter to Abigail Adams
July 3, 1776

TO-MORROW MORNING, Dr. Franklin, Mr. Rutledge and your humble servant set off to see that rare curiosity, Lord Howe. Do not imagine from this that a panic has spread to Philadelphia. By no means. This is only a refinement in policy.

—Letter to Samuel Adams
September 8, 1776

POSTERITY! You will never know, how much it cost the present Generation, to preserve your Freedom! I hope you will make a good use of it. If you do not, I shall repent in Heaven, that I ever took half the Pains to preserve it.

—Letter to Abigail Adams
April 26, 1777

IT SEEMS TO BE THE INTENTION OF HEAVEN, that We should be taught the full Value of our Liberty by the dearness of the Purchase, and the Importance of public Virtue by the Necessity of it.

—Letter to Abigail Adams
November 6, 1778

YOU KNOW PERFECTLY WELL that the enemy in America are at present very weak and in great distress in every part. They are weak in Canada, weak in Halifax, weak in Rhode Island, weak in New York, weak in the Floridas, and weak in every one of the West India Islands.

—Letter to Marquis de Lafayette
February 21, 1779

I CAN STATE A VERY SHORT ARGUMENT, that appears to me a demonstration upon French and Spanish principles alone, that it is more for their interest to employ their naval forces in America than in Europe.

—*Letter to John Jay*
May 13, 1780

YOU WILL SEE, the American Cause has had a signal Tryumph in this Country. If this had been the only Action of my Life, it would have been a Life well spent.

—*Letter to Abigail Adams*
July 1, 1782

I WILL VENTURE TO SAY, however feebly I may have acted my Part, or whatever Mistakes I may have committed, yet the Situations I have been in, between angry Nations and more angry actions, have been some of the most singular and interesting that ever happened to any Man. The fury of Ennemies as well as of Elements, the Subtlety and Arrogance of Allies and, what has been worse than all, the jealously, Envy, and little Pranks of Friends and CoPatriots, would be one of the most instructive Lessons in Morals and Politics that ever was committed to paper.

—*Diary of John Adams*
December 26, 1782

I DO NOT BELIEVE YOU could possibly have obtained a better treaty with America. On the contrary, the least delay would have lost you some advantages which you now have.

—*Letter to Benjamin Vaughan*
March 11, 1783

AS TO THE LOAN IN HOLLAND, I have never troubled you nor any one else with details of the vexations of various kinds which I met in the negotiation of it; indeed I never thought it prudent or safe to do it.

—*Letter to Robert Morris*
May 21, 1783

THE KING [GEORGE III], I really think, is the most accomplished courtier in his dominions. With all the affability of Charles II, he has all the domestic virtues and regularity of conduct as Charles I. He is the greatest talker in the world, and has a tenacious memory, stored with resources of small talk concerning all the little things of life which are inexhaustible. But so much of his time is, and has been consumed in this, that he is, on all the great affairs of society and government, as weak, as far as I can judge, as we understood him to be in America. He is also as obstinate. The unbounded popularity, acquired by his temperance and facetiousness, added to the splendor of his dignity, gives him such a continual feast of flattery, that he thinks all he does is right; and he pursues his own ideas with a firmness which would become the best system of action.

—*Letter to John Jay*
December 3, 1785

THE WORLD GROWS MORE ENLIGHTENED. Knowledge is more equally diffused. Newspapers, magazines, and circulating libraries have made mankind wiser. Titles and distinctions, ranks and orders, parade and ceremony, are all going out of fashion. This is roundly and frequently asserted in the streets, and sometimes on theatres of higher *rank*. Some truth is in it; and if the opportunity were temperately improved, to the reformation of abuses, the rectification of errors, and the dissipation of pernicious prejudices, a great advantage it might be. But, on the other hand, false inferences may be drawn from it, which may make mankind wish for the age of dragons, giants, and fairies.

—Discourses on Davila
April 1790–1791

BUT OLD AS I AM, war is, even to me, less dreadful than iniquity or diserved disgrace.

—*Letter to Henry Knox*
March 30, 1797

WHEN, AFTER FIFTEEN YEARS' EXERTION of all my faculties, and the faculties of all my friends, to bring the English nation to hearken to reason and respect justice, on the 19th of April, 1775, I found hostilities commenced and the blood of our citizens barbarously split, I concluded what I had long foreseen—that we must resist in arms the whole force of the British empire.

—*Letter to Mercy Otis Warren*
July 20, 1807

THE WINDS BEGAN TO RUSTLE, the clouds gather, it grows dark; will these airy forces rear up the Ocean to a foaming fury? A spirit seems to be rising; a spirit of contrition and shame at our long apathy and lethargy; a spirit of resentment of injuries, a spirit of indignation at insolence; and what to me is very remarkable, a spirit of greater unanimity than I have ever witnessed in this country for fifty years.

—Letter to Richard Rush
October 8, 1813

YOU "NEVER PROFOUNDLY ADMIRED Mr. Hancock. He had vanity and caprice." I can say, with truth, that I profoundly admired him, and more profoundly loved him. If he had vanity and caprice, so had I.

—Letter to William Tudor
June 1, 1817

THE AMERICAN REVOLUTION was not a common event. Its effects and consequences have already been awful over a great part of the globe. And when and where are they to cease? But what do we mean be the American Revolution? Do we mean the American war? The Revolution was effected before the war commenced. The Revolution was in the minds and hearts of the people; a change in their religious sentiments of their duties and obligations...The radical change in the principles, opinions, sentiments, and affections of the people, was the real American Revolution.

—Letter to Hezekiah Niles
February 13, 1818

THE COMMITTEE MET, discussed the subject, and then appointed Mr. Jefferson and me to make the draught, I suppose because we were the two first on the list.

The sub-committee met. Jefferson proposed to me to make the draught. I said "I will not."

"You should do it."

"Oh! No."

"Why will you not. You ought to do it."

"I will not."

"Why?"

"Reasons enough."

"What can be your reasons?"

"Reason first—you are a Virginian, and a Virginian ought to appear at the head of this business. Reason second—I am obnoxious, suspected, and unpopular. You are very much otherwise. Reason third—You can write ten times better than I can."

"Well," said Jefferson, "if you are decided, I will do as well as I can.

—Diary of John Adams
August 6, 1822

THE PRESET FEEBLE STATE OF MY HEALTH will not indulge the hope of participation with more than my best wishes, in the joys, and festivities and solemn services of that day, on which will be completed the fiftieth year from the birth of the independence of the United States. A memorable epoch in the annals of the human race, destined in future history to form the brightest or the blackest page, according to the use or the abuse of those political institutions by which they shall, in time to come, be shaped by the human mind.

—Reply to an invitation to 50th Independence Day celebrations from a committee of the citizens of Quincy, Massachusetts
June 7, 1826

ADAMS ON GOVERNMENT

What is the function of government and how should a new one be framed? How much power should be given to an executive and how could that power be controlled? How do you create a government of laws and not of men in order to avoid the abuses of power the British government demonstrated in the 1750s and beyond? What is the role of the federal government as opposed to state and local government? Are we to trust people or institutions? How do you balance rights and responsibilities, the role of the few and the many, the executive and the legislative body? How do you separate powers in order to avoid dictatorship? To Adams, these questions were at the heart of freedom, and he wrote extensively of their importance. In 1780 he would go on to write the Massachusetts Constitution and later to defend the American Constitution, using his own experiences and theories of government as one of his most valuable resources.

MAN HAS CERTAINLY AN EXALTED SOUL; and the same principle in human nature,—that aspiring, noble principle founded in benevolence, and cherished by knowledge; I mean the love of power, which has been so often the cause of slavery,—has, whenever freedom has existed, been the cause of freedom.

—A Dissertation on the Canon and the Feudal Law
1765

THE JAWS OF POWER are always opened to devour, and her arm is always stretched out, if possible, to destroy the freedom of thinking, speaking, and writing.

—A Dissertation on the Canon and Feudal Law
1765

THE TRUE SOURCE OF OUR SUFFERINGS has been our timidity. We have been afraid to think. We have felt a reluctance to examining into the grounds of our privileges, and the extent in which we have an indisputable right to demand them, against all the power and authority on earth.

—A Dissertation on the Canon and the Feudal Law
1765

LIBERTY CANNOT BE PRESERVED without a general knowledge among the people, who have a right, from the frame of their nature, to knowledge as their great Creator, who does nothing in vain, has given them understandings, and a desire to know; but besides this, they have a right, an indisputable, unalienable, indefeasible, divine right to that most dreaded and envied kind of knowledge, I mean, of the characters and conduct of their rulers.

—A Dissertation on the Canon and the Feudal Law
1765

LET EVERY SLUICE of knowledge be opened and set a-flowing.

—A Dissertation on the Canon and Feudal Law
1765

THERE IS DANGER FROM ALL MEN. The only maxim of a free government ought to be to trust no man living with power to endanger the public liberty.

—Notes for an oration at Braintree, Massachusetts
Spring 1772

EVERY MAN IN IT IS A GREAT MAN, an orator, a Critick, a statesman and therefore every Man upon every Question must shew his oratory, his Criticism and his Political Abilities.

—Letter to Abigail Adams
October 9, 1774

METAPHYSICIANS AND POLITICIANS may dispute forever, but they will never find any other moral principle or foundation of rule or obedience, than the consent of governors and governed.

— "Novanglus" essay printed in the Boston Gazette, *no. 7*
1775

A GOVERNMENT OF LAWS, AND NOT OF MEN.

— "Novanglus" essay printed in the Boston Gazette, *no. 7*
1775
and also incorporated into the Massachusetts Constitution
1780

A CONSTITUTION OF GOVERNMENT once changed from Freedom, can never be restored. Liberty, once lost, is lost forever.

—*Letter to Abigail Adams*
July 7, 1775

I AGREE WITH YOU that in politics the middle way is none at all. If we finally fall in this great and glorious Contest, it will be by bewildering ourselves in groping after the middle Way

—*Letter to Horatio Gates*
March 23, 1776

NOTHING IS MORE CERTAIN from the history of nations and nature of man, than that some forms of government are better fitted for being well administered that others.

We ought to consider what is the end of government, before we determine which is the best form. Upon this point all speculative politicians will agree, that the happiness of society is the end of government, as all divines and moral philosophers will agree that the happiness of the individual is the end of man. From this principle it will follow, that the form of government which communicates ease, comfort, security, or, in one word, happiness, to the greatest number of persons, and in the greatest degree, is the best.

—Thoughts on Government
March–April 1776

AS GOOD GOVERNMENT IS AN EMPIRE OF LAWS, how shall your laws be made? In a large society, inhabiting an extensive country, it is impossible that the whole should assemble to make laws. The first necessary step, then, is to depute power from the many to a few of the most wise and good.

—Thoughts on Government
March–April 1776

TO AVOID THESE DANGERS, let a distinct assembly be constituted, as a mediator between the two extreme branches of the legislature, that which represents the people, and that which is vested with the executive power.

—Thoughts on Government
March–April 1776

THE DIGNITY AND STABILITY OF GOVERNMENT in all its branches, the morals of the people, and every blessing of society depend so much upon an upright and skilful administration of justice, that the judicial power ought to be distinct from both the legislative and executive, and independent upon both, that so it may be a check upon both, as both should be checks upon that. The judges, therefore, should be always men of learning and experience in the laws, of exemplary morals, great patience, calmness, coolness, and attention.

—Thoughts on Government
March–April 1776

I HAVE REASONS TO BELIEVE that no Colony, which shall assume a Government under the People, will give it up. There is something very unnatural and odious in a Government 1000 Leagues off. An whole Government of our own Choice, managed by Persons whom We love, revere, and can confide in, has charms in it for which Men will fight.

—Letter to Abigail Adams
May 17, 1776

OUR FOREIGN AFFAIRS, are like to be in future as they have been in times past an eternal Scæne of Faction. The fluctuation of Councils at Philadelphia have encouraged it, and even good Men Seem to be Seized with the Spirit of it.

—Letter to Abigail Adams
March 28, 1783

THE PROJECT OF A NEW CONSTITUTION, has Objections against it, to which I find it difficult to reconcile my self, but I am so unfortunate as to differ somewhat from you in the Articles, according to your last kind Letter.

You are afraid of the one—I, of the few. We agree perfectly that the many should have a full fair and perfect Representation.—You are Apprehensive of Monarchy; I, of Aristocracy. I would therefore have given more Power to the President and less to the Senate. The Nomination and Appointment to all offices I would have given to the President, assisted only by a Privy Council of his own Creation, but not a Vote or Voice would I have given to the Senate or any Senator, unless he were of the Privy Council. Faction and Distraction are the sure and certain Consequence of giving to a Senate a vote in the distribution of offices.

You are apprehensive the President when once chosen, will be chosen again and again as long as he lives. So much the better as it appears to me.—You are apprehensive of foreign Interference, Intrigue, Influence. So am I.—But, as often as Elections happen, the danger of foreign Influence recurs. The less frequently they happen the less danger.—And if the Same Man may be chosen again, it is probable he will be, and the danger of foreign Influence will be less. Foreigners, seeing little Prospect will have less Courage for Enterprize.

Elections, my dear sir, Elections to offices which are great objects of Ambition, I look at with terror. Experiments of this kind have been so often tryed, and so universally found productive of Horrors, that there is great Reason to dread them.

—Letter to Thomas Jefferson
December 6, 1787

PUBLIC BUSINESS MY SON, must always be done by Somebody or other. If wise men decline it others will not. If honest men refuse it, others will not...My advice to my children, is to maintain an independent Character, though in poverty and obscurity: neither riches nor illustr[ation] will console a man under the reflection that he has acted a mean, mercenary part, much less, a dishonest one.

—Letter to Thomas Boylston Adams
September 2, 1789

THERE IS NOTHING WHICH I DREAD SO MUCH as a division of the republic into great parties, each arranged under its leader, and concerning measure in opposition to each other. This, in my humble apprehension, is to be dreaded as the greatest political evil under our Constitution.

—*Letter to Jonathan Jackson*
October 2, 1789

HAS THERE EVER BEEN A NATION WHO UNDERSTOOD the human heart better than the Romans, or made a better use of the passion for consideration, congratulation, and distinction? They considered that, as reason is the guide of life, the senses, the imagination and the affections are the springs of activity.

—Discourses on Davila
April 1790–April 1791

AS THE PRIDE OF WEALTH PRODUCED nothing but meanness of sentiment and a sordid scramble for money; and the pride of birth produced some degree of emulation in knowledge and virtue; the wisdom of nations has endeavored to employ one prejudice to counteract another; the prejudice in favor of birth, to moderate, correct, and restrain the prejudice in favor of wealth.

—Discourses on Davila
April 1790–April 1791

BAD MEN INCREASE IN KNOWLEDGE as fast as good men; and science, arts, taste, sense, and letters, are employed for the purposes of injustice and tyranny, as well as those of law and liberty; for corruption, as well as for virtue.

—Discourses on Davila
April 1790–April 1791

THE EXECUTIVE AND THE LEGISLATIVE POWERS are natural rivals; and if each has not an effectual control over the other, the weaker will ever be the lamb in the paws of the wolf. The nation which will not adopt an equilibrium of power must adopt a despotism.

—Discourses on Davila
April 1790–April 1791

MY COUNTRY HAS IN ITS WISDOM CONTRIVED for me the most insignificant office [the vice-presidency] that ever the invention of man contrived or his imagination conceived and as I can do neither good nor evil, I must be borne away by others and meet the common Fate.

—*Letter to Abigail Adams*
December 19, 1791

THE NOISE OF ELECTION IS OVER, and I have the Consolation to find that all the States which are fœderal have been unanimous for me, and all those in which the Antifœderalists were the predominant Party, unanimous against me: from whence my Vanity concludes that both Parties think me decidedly fœderal and of Some consequence.

—Letter to Abigail Adams
December 28, 1792

I AM AFRAID THAT HAMILTONS SCHEMES will become unpopular, because the State Legislatures are undermining them and Congress will be obliged either to let them fall in the Publick opinion, or to support them by measures which will be unpopular. Hamilton has been intemperately puffed and this has excited green Eyed Jealousy and haggard Envy. Jays Friends have let Escape feelings of Jealousy as well as Jeffersons. And it is very natural. Poor me who have no Friends to be jealous, I am left out of the Question and pray I ever may.

—Letter to Abigail Adams
February 17, 1793

BY THE LAW OF NATURE, all Men are Men and not Eagles, That is they are all of the same Species. And this is the most that the Equality of Nature amounts to. But Man differs by Nature from Man, almost as much as Man from Beast. The Equality of Nature is Moral and Political only and means that all Men are independent. But a Physical Inequality, an Intellectual Inequality of the most serious kind is established unchangeably by the Author of Nature. And Society has a Right to establish any other Inequalities it may judge necessary for its good.

—Letter to Abigail Adams
February 4, 1794

WHEN IT WAS FIRST PERCEIVED, in early times, that no middle course for America remained between unlimited submission to a foreign legislature and a total independence of its claims, men of reflection were less apprehensive of danger from the formidable power of fleets and armies they must determine to resist them, from the contests and dissensions, which would certainly arise, concerning the forms of government to be instituted, over the whole, and over the parts of this extensive country. Relying, however on the purity of their intentions, the justice of their cause, and the integrity and intelligence of the people, under an overruling Providence, which had so signally protected the country from the first, the representatives of the nation, consisting of little more than half its present number, not only broke to pieces the chains which were forging and the rod of iron that was lifted up, but frankly cut asunder the ties which had bound them, and launched into an ocean of uncertainty.

—Inaugural address
March 4, 1797

THE COMMERCE OF THE UNITED STATES is essential, if not to their existence, at least to their comfort, their growth, prosperity, and happiness. The genius, character, and habits of the people are highly commercial. The cities have been formed and exist upon commerce. Our agriculture, fisheries, arts, and manufactures are connected with and depend upon it. In short, commerce has made this country what it is, and it cannot be destroyed or neglected without involving the people in poverty and distress.

—First annual address
November 22, 1797

IN ORDER TO SAVE YOU THE TROUBLE and Expence of purchasing Horses and Carriages, which will not be necessary, I have to inform you that I shall leave in the stables of the United States seven Horses and two Carriages with Harness and Property of the United States. These may not be suitable for you: but they will certainly save you a considerable Expence as they belong to the studd of the President's Household. I have the honor to be with great respect Sir your most obedient and humble servant.

—Letter to Thomas Jefferson
February 20, 1801

WILL ANY PHILOSOPHER SAY, that beauty has no influence in human society? If he does, let him read the histories of Eve, Judith, Helen, the fair Gabrielle, Diana of Poitiers, Pompadour, Du Barry, Susanna, Abigail, Lady Hamilton, Mrs. Clark, and a million others. Are not despots, monarchs, aristocrats, and democrats, equally liable to be seduced by beauty to confer favors and influence suffrages?

—Letter to John Taylor
April 15, 1814

THAT ALL MEN ARE BORN TO EQUAL RIGHTS IS TRUE. Every being has a right to his own, as clear, as moral, as sacred, as any other being has. This is as indubitable as a moral government in the universe. But to teach that all men are born with equal powers and faculties, to equal influence in society, to equal property and advantages through life, is as gross a fraud, as glaring an imposition on the credulity of the people, as ever was practised by monks, by Druids, by Brahmins, by priests of the immortal Lama, or by the self-styled philosophers of the French revolution.

—Letter to John Taylor
April 15, 1814

WHEN SUPERIOR GENIUS GIVES GREATER INFLUENCE in society than is possessed by inferior genius, or a mediocrity of genius, that is, than by the ordinary level of men, this superior influence I call natural aristocracy. This cause, you say, is "fluctuating." What then? it is aristocracy still, while it exists. And is not democracy "fluctuating" too? Are the waves of the sea, or the winds of the air, or the gossamer that idles in the wanton summer air, more fluctuating that democracy? While I admit the existence of democracy, notwithstanding its instability, you must acknowledge that existence of natural aristocracy, notwithstanding its fluctuations.

—*Letter to John Taylor*
1814

WHEN MY SON DEPARTED FOR RUSSIA, I enjoyed it upon him to write nothing to me, which he was not willing to be published in French and English newspapers. He has very scrupulously observed this rule.

—*Letter to James Madison*
November 28, 1814

AS I HAVE ALWAYS BEEN CONVINCED, that abuse of words has been the great instrument of sophistry and chicanery, of party, faction, and division of society, the time has been when I would have attended you with pleasure in your pursuit of correct definitions.

—*Letter to J. H. Tiffany*
March 31, 1819

NO MAN WHO EVER HELD THE OFFICE OF PRESIDENT would congratulate a friend on obtaining it. He will make one man ungrateful and a hundred men his enemies, for every office he can bestow.

—Reported by Josiah Quincy III
February 14, 1825

Adams on Farming

For its first two centuries, the United States was a rural nation. John Adams's father was a farmer, as had been previous generations of the Adams family. John Adams read extensively on agriculture and discussed ideas with neighbors. The farm in Quincy provided a livelihood to the family and was managed by Abigail while John was absent on his frequent travels. In 1801 he retired to the farm, his books, and his correspondence.

MY THOUGHTS HAVE TAKEN a sudden turn to husbandry. Have contracted with Jo. Field to clear my swamp, and to build me a long string of stone wall, and with Isaac to build me sixteen rods more and with Jo Field to build me six rods more. And my thoughts are running continually from the orchard to the pasture and from thence to the swamp, and thence to the house and barn and land adjoining. Sometimes I am at the orchard ploughing up acre after acre and planting, pruning apple trees, mending fences, carting dung; sometimes in the pasture, digging stones, clearing bushes, pruning trees, building wall to redeem posts and rails; and sometimes removing button trees down to my house; sometimes I am at the old swamp, burning bushes, digging stumps and roots, cutting ditches, across the meadow, and against my uncle; and am sometimes at the other end of the town, buying posts and rails, to fence against my uncle, and against the brook; and am sometimes ploughing the upland, with six yoke of oxen, and planting corn, potatoes, &c. and digging up the meadow and sowing onions, planting cabbages &c. &c.

—Diary of John Adams
October 24, 1762

HERE IS SOLITUDE AND RETIREMENT. Still, calm, and serene. Cool, tranquil and peaceful. The cell of the hermit; Out at one window you see Mount Wollaston, the first seat of our Ancestors, and beyond that Stony Field Hill, covered over with corn and fruits. At the other window, an orchard and beyond that the large marsh called the broad meadows.

—Diary of John Adams
August 14, 1769

I BELIEVE IT IS TIME to think a little about my Family and Farm. The fine Weather, we have had for 8 or 10 days past I hope has been carefully improved to get in my Hay. It is a great Mortification to me that I could not attend every step of their Progress in mowing, making and carting. I long to see what Burden—But I long more still to see to the procuring more Sea Weed and Marsh Mud and sand &c."

—Letter to Abigail Adams
July 6, 1774

WE HAVE HAD GREEN PEAS, this Week past, but they were brought over the River from New Jersey, to this Markett. There are none grown in the City, or on the West side of the River yet. The Reason is, the Soil of New Jersey is a warm Sand, that of Pensilvania, a cold Clay. So much for Peas and Berries.

—Letter to Abigail Adams
June 2, 1776

THE SPRING ADVANCES, very rapidly, and all Nature will soon be cloathed in her gayest Robes. The green Grass, which begins to shew itself, here, and there, revives in my longing Imagination my little Farm, and its dear Inhabitants. What Pleasures has not this vile War, deprived me of? I want to wander, in my Meadows, to ramble over my Mountains, and to sit in Solitude, or with her who has all my Heart, by the side of the Brooks...

I long for rural and domestic scænes, for the warbling of Birds and the Prattle of my Children. Dont you think I am somewhat poetical this morning, for one of my Years, and considering the Gravity, and Insipidity of my Employment.—As much as I converse with Sages and Heroes, they have very little of my Love or Admiration. I should prefer the Delights of a Garden to the Dominion of a World. I have nothing of Caesars Greatness in my soul. Power, has not my Wishes in her Train. The Gods, by granting me Health, and Peace and Competence, the Society of my Family and Friends, the Perusal of my Books, and the Enjoyment of my Farm and Garden, would make me as happy as my Nature and State will bear.

—*Letter to Abigail Adams*
March 16, 1777

PRAY HOW DOES YOUR ASPARAGUS PERFORM?

—*Letter to Abigail Adams*
May 22, 1777

You go on in the Conduct of your Farm with so much spirit, amidst all your melancholly avocations, that it is a noble Regale to read your Letters. Plant the Ground which broke up last fall with corn. Sow Barley where We had corn last Year. Plant again the lower Garden. Potatoes again at the Beach Meadow. Plant again Farons last Years Corn field. Buy as many cows and young Stock as you can keep in plenty. Send the sheep as soon as convenient to the Pasture by Harmans.

—Letter to Abigail Adams
March 11, 1794

I have spent my Summer so deliciously in farming that I return to the old Story of Politicks with great Reluctance. The Earth is grateful. You find it so, I dare say.

—Letter to Thomas Jefferson
November 21, 1794

I wish, if it is possible, that our Men, after carting out the Manure upon the old Clover at home, would cart out that whole heap of limed manure in Mr Joys Cowyard, upon Quincys Meadow, as well as the heap already in the Meadow. These two heaps will give the Meadow a good dressing.

—Letter to Abigail Adams
December 6, 1795

MR. MEREDITH, at Mr. Vaughan's explained to me his method. He takes a first crop of clover early: then breaks up the ground, cross ploughs and harrows it; then plants potatoes. He only ploughs a furrow, drops the potatoes a foot asunder and then covers them with another furrow. He ploughs now and then between these rows: but never hoes. As soon as the season comes for sowing his winter barley. He digs the potatoes, ploughs and harrows the ground, sows the winter barley with clover seeds and orchard grass seeds; and the next spring he has a great crop of barley and afterwards a great burthen of grass.

—Diary of John Adams
June 21, 1795

YESTERDAY MOW'D ALL THE GRASS on Stony field Hill. To day ploughing for hilling among the corn over against the house. Briesler laying the foundation of the new barn which is to be raised tomorrow, at the east end of my father's barn.

—Diary of John Adams
July 12, 1796

THAT APPLE-TREE, OVER THE WAY, to which the Beauty and Convenience of the Road has been sacrificed for an hundred years, has now in its turn, with Apples enough upon [it] to make two Barrells of Cyder, fallen a Sacrifice to the Beauty and Convenience of the Road. It has been felled this morning, never to rise again and the Road is to be widened and enlarged.

—Diary of John Adams
February 21, 1796

A FINE DAY. I HAVE FINISHED PETRARCH. Walked up to the new Barn and over to the old Plain. Sullivan and Mr. Sam. Hayward threshing—Billings and Bass carting Earth and Seaweed and liming the Compost. Mr. Wilbert dined with Us. James brought home the oxen from Long Island. Trash burning Bushes in the Swamp on Pennis Hill.

—*Diary of John Adams*
August 5, 1796

TEN YOKE OF OXEN AND TWELVE HANDS ploughing in the meadow. It is astonishing that such a Meadow should have lain so long in such a State. Brakes, Hassock Grass, Cranberry Vines, Poke or Skunk Cabbage, Button Bushes, alder Bushes, old Stumps and Roots, Rocks, Turtles, Eels, Frogs were the Chief Things to be found in it. But I presume it may be made to produce Indian and English Grain, and English Grass, especially Herdsgrass in Abundance. At least the beauty of the Meadow and the Sweetness of it and the Air over it will be improved.

—*Diary of John Adams*
August 19, 1796

I HAD HEARD MY FATHER SAY that he never knew a piece of land [to] run away or break.

—*Autobiography of John Adams*
1802–1807

Adams on Science and Technology

In the eighteenth century, an educated person learned science as well as the classics. John Adams studied science at Harvard, and his library contained many books on the subject, as well as books on mathematics. In 1779 he proposed that the American Academy of Arts and Science be established, and he was elected its president from 1791 to 1813.

WE HAD A VERY SEVERE SHOCK OF AN EARTHQUAKE. It continued near four minutes. I was then at my father's house in Braintree, and woke out of my sleep in the midst of it. The house seemed to rock and reel and crash, as if it would fall in ruins about us. Chimneys were shattered by it within one mile of my father's house.

—Diary of John Adams
November 18, 1755

IN LIKE MANNER WE, WHO SEE BUT A FEW COGS in one wheel of the great machine of the universe, can make no right judgment of particular phenomena in nature.

—Diary of John Adams
May 4, 1756

THE REASONING OF MATHEMATICIANS is founded on certain and infallible principles. Every word they use conveys a determinate idea, and by accurate definitions they excite the same ideas in the mind of the reader that were in the mind of the writer.

—Diary of John Adams
June 1, 1756

IT WILL BE EASY FOR ANY MAN to conclude that a Man whose youth and spirits and strength, have been spent in Husbandry, Merchandise, Politicks, nay in science or Literature, will never master so immense and involved a science: for it may be taken for a never-failing Maxim, that Youth is the only Time for laying the Foundation of a great Improvement in any science or Profession, and that an Application in advanced Years, after the Mind is crowded, the Attention divided, or dissipated, and the memory in part lost will make but a tolerable Artist at best.

—Diary of John Adams
November 11, 1759

I HAVE SEEN THE UTILITY OF GEOMETRY, Geography, and the Art of drawing so much of late, that I must intreat you, my dear, to teach the Elements of those Sciences to my little Girl and Boys.

—Letter to Abigail Adams
September 26, 1775

WHAT IS THIS GULF STREAM? What is the course of it? from what point, and to what point does it flow? how broad is it? how far distant is it from the continent of America? What is the longitude and latitude of it?

—Diary and Autobiography of John Adams
February 28, 1778

AFTER DINNER WE WENT TO THE ACADEMY OF SCIENCES, and heard Mr. d'Alembert, as perpetual secretary, pronounce eulogies on several of their members, lately deceased. Voltaire and Franklin were both present, and there presently arose a general cry that M. Voltaire and M. Franklin should be introduced to each other.

—Diary and Autobiography of John Adams
April 29, 1778

RITTENHOUSE WAS A VIRTUOUS AND AMIABLE MAN; an exquisite Mechanician; Master of the Astronomy known in his time; an expert Mathematician, a patient calculator of Numbers.

—Letter to Thomas Jefferson
March 3, 1814

AS YOU KNOW I HAVE OFTEN BEEN AMBITIOUS of introducing to your acquaintance some of our literary characters. I now send you in the same spirit, some mathematical papers by our Mr. Bowditch, who has translated La Place's mechanique coeliste and has written commentaries upon it as voluminous as the book, which are thought by our scientific people to be one of the greatest astronomical productions of the present age: I hope the public will soon see it in print. I would write you news if I had any, but this is "the piping time of peace." I am as ever your friend and humble servant.

—Letter to Thomas Jefferson
February 19, 1819

Adams on Education

At the age of sixteen, John Adams began his college education at Harvard and graduated four years later, in 1755. His father had wanted him to become a clergyman, but after teaching in Worcester, he decided on a career in the law. He was admitted to the Suffolk County Bar in 1758, at the age of twenty-three. The Continental Congress twice sent Adams to Europe on diplomatic missions. Because he and Abigail wanted their sons to see more of the world than the average New Englander, he took his son John Quincy with him on the first trip, and on the next he took both John Quincy and Charles. The boys were educated by tutors and at the University of Leyden, Netherlands. Later, in the mid-1780s, all of his sons—John Quincy, Charles, and Thomas Boylston—followed their father's footsteps and entered Harvard.

I SOMETIMES, IN MY SPRIGHTLY MOMENTS consider myself, in my great chair at school, as some dictator at the head of a common-wealth. In this little state I can discover all the great geniuss, all the surprizing actions and revolutions of the great world, in miniature.

—Diary and Autobiography of John Adams
March 15, 1756

'TIS IMPOSSIBLE TO EMPLOY WITH FULL ADVANTAGES the forces of our minds in study, in council, or in argument, whither examining with great attention and exactness all our mental facilities in all their operations, as explained by writers on the human understanding.

—Letter to Jonathan Sewall
October 1759

A NATIVE OF AMERICA WHO CANNOT READ AND WRITE is as rare an appearance as a Jacobite or a Roman Catholic, that is, as rare as a comet or an earthquake.

—A Dissertation on the Canon and the Feudal Law
1765

I WISH I UNDERSTOOD FRENCH AS WELL AS YOU. I would have gone to Canada, if I had. I feel the want of education every Day— particularly of that Language. I pray My dear, that you would not suffer your Sons or your Daughter, ever to feel a similar Pain.

—Letter to Abigail Adams
February 18, 1776

LAWS FOR THE LIBERAL EDUCATION OF YOUTH, especially of the lower class of people, are so extremely wise and useful, that, to a humane and generous mind, no expense for this purpose would be thought extravagant.

—Thoughts on Government
March–April 1776

EARLY YOUTH IS THE TIME, to learn the Arts and Sciences, and especially to correct the Ear, and the Imagination, by forming a Style...

The Faculty of Writing is attainable, by Art, Practice, and Habit only. The sooner, therefore the Practice begins, the more likely it will be to succeed. Have no Mercy upon an affected Phrase, any more than an affected Air, Gate, Dress, or Manners.

—Letter to Abigail Adams
July 7, 1776

THE FOUNDATIONS OF NATIONAL MORALITY must be laid in private families. In vain are schools, academies, and universities, instituted, if loose principles and licentious habits are impressed upon children in their earliest years. The mothers are the earliest and most important instructors of youth.

—Diary and Autobiography of John Adams
June 7, 1778

THE SCIENCE OF GOVERNMENT it is my duty to study, more than all other sciences; the Arts of Legislation and Administration and Negotiation ought to take place, indeed to exclude in a manner all other arts. I must study Politics and War, that my sons may have liberty to study Mathematics and Philosophy. My sons ought to study Mathematics and Philosophy, Geography, natural History, Naval Architectures, navigation, Commerce and Agriculture in order to give their Children a right to study Painting, Poetry, Music, Architecture, Statuary, Tapestry and Porcelain.

—Letter to Abigail Adams
May 12, 1780

AMIDST YOUR ARDOUR FOR GREEK AND LATIN I hope you will not forget your mother Tongue. Read Somewhat in the English Poets every day...You will never be alone, with a Poet in your Poket. You will never have an idle Hour.

—Letter to John Quincy Adams
May 14, 1781

HE [JOHN QUINCY ADAMS] IS ANXIOUS to study some time at your university before he begins the study of the law, which appears at the present to be the profession of his choice. He must undergo an examination in which I suspect he will not appear exactly what he is. In truth, there are few who take their degree at college, who have so much knowledge. But his studies having been pursued by himself on his travels, without any steady tutor, he will be found awkward in speaking Latin.

—Letter to Benjamin Waterhouse
April 24, 1785

I BEGIN TO DOUBT WHETHER I WAS IN THE WAY of my Duty in ever engaging in public Life. With my Family of Children ought I not to have staid at home, minded their Education and sought their Advancement in Life! It is too late for this Cemistry now.

—Letter to Abigail Adams
December 17, 1798

EDUCATION, which you brought into View in one of your letters, is a Subject so vast, and the System of Writers are so various and so contradictory: that human Life is too short to examine it; and a Man must die before he can learn to bring up his Children.

—Letter to Thomas Jefferson
June 19, 1815

ADAMS ON BOOKS
AND LIBRARIES

John Adams was an avid reader from an early age. He read extensively on many subjects, including literature, the classics, philosophy, religion, science, agriculture, law, economics, and others. His books were in English, French, Greek, Italian, Latin, and Spanish, and over the course of his life he built a valuable collection. He wrote to others about books he had read and had a lengthy correspondence with the authors Mercy Otis Warren and John Taylor about why, in his view, their writings on history had not been accurate. Adams often covered the margins of his books with his own commentary, and his personal notes give insight into what he thought about the words of other authors. At the age of eighty-six, he arranged to donate his personal library, an "estate of books," to the city of Quincy, Massachusetts. The library was transferred to the Boston Public Library in 1894. His books and papers have become an important window into the past, and a more valuable estate than he could ever have guessed.

READING MILTON. That man's soul, it seems to me, was distended as wide as creation. His power over the human mind was absolute and unlimited. His genius was great beyond conception, and his learning without bounds.

—*Diary of John Adams*
April 30, 1756

YESTERDAY AND TODAY I HAVE READ LOUD, Tully's four Orations against Cataline. The sweetness and grandeur of his sounds, and the harmony of his numbers, give pleasure enough to reward the reading if one understood none of his meaning. Besides I find it, a noble exercise. It exercises my lungs, raises my spirits, opens my porr[s], quickens the circulations, and so contributes much to health.

—Diary of John Adams
December 21, 1758

I BEGAN POPE'S HOMER, last Saturday night a week and last night, which was Monday night I finished it. Thus I found that in seven days I could have easily read the six volumes…Therefore I will be bound that in six months I will conquer him in Greek, and make myself able to translate every line in him elegantly.

—Diary of John Adams
August 19, 1760

I WALKED TO THE BOOKSELLERS, Stockdale, Cadel, Dilly, Almon and met Dr. Priestly for the first time.

—Diary and Autobiography of John Adams
April 19, 1786

I READ MY EYES OUT and can't read half enough…The more one reads the more one sees we have to read.

—Letter to Abigail Adams
December 28, 1794

AS MY PARENTS WERE BOTH FOND OF READING, and my father has destined his first born, long before his birth to a public Education, I was very early taught to read at home and at a school of Mrs. Belcher.

—Autobiography of John Adams
1802–1807

THE PSALMS OF DAVID, in Sublimity beauty, pathos and Originality, or in one Word, in poetry, are superiour to all the Odes Hymns and Songs in any language. But I had rather read them in our prose translation, than in any version I have seen. His morality, however, often shocks me, like Tristram Shandy's execrations.

—Letter to Thomas Jefferson
November 14, 1813

I HAVE READ CHAUTEAUBRIAD, with as much delight, as I have read Bunyan['s] Pilgrims Progress, Robinson Crusoes Travels or Gullivers; or Whitefields; or Westleys Life; or the Life of St. Francis, St. Anthony or St. Ignatius Loyaula.

—Letter to Thomas Jefferson
December 13, 1813

I HAVE EXAMINED ALL RELIGIONS, as well as my narrow Sphere, my straightened means and my busy life, would allow me; and the results is the Bible is the best book in the World. It contains more of my little philosophy than all the libraries I have seen.

—Letter to Thomas Jefferson
December 25, 1813

I am very glad you have seriously read Plato: and still more rejoiced to find that your reflections upon him so perfectly harmonize with mine. Some thirty Years ago I took upon me the severe task of going through all his Works. With the help of two Latin Translations, and one English and one French Translation and comparing some of the most remarkable passages with the Greek, I labored through the tedious toil.

—Letter to Thomas Jefferson
July 16, 1814

I have been a Lover and a Reader of Romances all my life. From Don Quixotte and Gill Blas to the Scottish chiefs and an hundred others.

—Letter to Thomas Jefferson
December 12, 1816

My Friends or Enemies continue to overwhelm me with Books. Whatever may be their intentions, charitable or otherwise, they certainly contribute, to continue me to vegetate, much as I have done for the Sixteen Years last past.

—Letter to Thomas Jefferson
May 18, 1817

ADAMS ON RELIGION
AND RELIGIOUS FREEDOM

Early in his life, at the urging of his father, John Adams contemplated becoming a clergyman, but after the Great Awakening made him question whether that was the best career for him, he turned to law and politics He read extensively on religion, studying all creeds and authors and often corresponding with others about the subject. As he wrote to Thomas Jefferson on April 19, 1817, "Without religion this World would be Something not fit to be mentioned in polite company."

SPENT AN HOUR IN THE BEGINNING of the evening at Major Gardiners, where it was thought that the design of Christianity was not to make men good Riddle Solvers or good mystery mongers, but good men, good magistrates, and good subjects, good husbands and good wives, good parents and good children, good masters and good servants.

—*Diary of John Adams*
February 18, 1756

HONESTY, SINCERITY AND OPENNESS, I ESTEEM essential marks of a good mind. I am therefore, of opinion, that men ought, (after they have examined with unbiased judgments, every system of religion, and chosen one system, on their own authority, for themselves) to avow their opinions and defend them with boldness.

—*Diary and Autobiography of John Adams*
March 7, 1756

NOTHING CAN PROCEED FROM NOTHING. But something can proceed from something, and thus the Deity produced this vast and beautiful frame of the universe out of nothing; that is, He had no preexistent matter to work upon, or to change from a chaos into a world. But He produced a world into being by his Almighty fiat, perhaps, in a manner analogous to the production of resolutions in our minds.

—Diary and Autobiography of John Adam
May 23, 1756

'TIS IMPOSSIBLE TO JUDGE with much Precision of the true Motives and Qualities of human Actions, or of the Propriety of Rules contrived to govern them, without considering with like Attention, all the Passions, Appetites, Affections in Nature from which they flow. An intimate Knowledge therefore of the intellectual and moral World is the whole foundation on which a stable structure of Knowledge can be erected.

—Letter to Jonathan Sewall
October 1759

DOES NOT NATURAL MORALITY, and much more Christian Benevolence, make it our indispensible Duty to lay ourselves out, to serve our fellow Creatures to the Utmost of our Power, in promoting and supporting those great Political systems, and general Regulations upon which the Happiness of Multitudes depends.

—Letter to Abigail Adams
October 29, 1775

LET THEM REVERE NOTHING but Religion, Morality and Liberty.

—Letter to Abigail Adams
April 15, 1776

WE SHOULD BEGIN BY SETTING CONSCIENCE FREE. When all men of all religions, consistent with morals and property...shall enjoy equal liberty, property or rather security of property and an equal chance for honors and power...we may expect that improvements will be made in the human character and the state of society.

—Letter to Dr. Richard Price
April 8, 1785

ONE GREAT ADVANTAGE OF THE CHRISTIAN RELIGION is, that it brings the great principle of the law of nature and nations—Love your neighbor as yourself, and to do to others that others should do to you,—to the knowledge, belief, and veneration of the whole people. Children, servants, women, and me, are all professors in the science of public and private morality.

—Diary of John Adams
August 14, 1796

AND MAY THAT BEING, who is supreme over all, the patron of order, the fountain of justice, and the protector, in all ages of the world, of virtuous liberty, continue his blessing upon this nation and its government, and give it all possible success and duration, consistent with the ends of his providence!

—Inaugural address
March 4, 1797

BENEVOLENCE AND BENEFICENCE, Industry, Equity and Humanity Resignation and submission, Repentance and Reformation are the essence of my Religion. Alas, how weakly and imperfectly have I fullfilled the Duties of my own Religion! I look back Upon a long Life very poorly Spent in my own Estimation.

—Letter to Abigail Adams
October 27, 1799

I HAVE MORE TO SAY, ON RELIGION. For more than sixty Years I have been attentive to this great Subject. Controversies, between Calvinists and Arminians, Trinitarians and Uniterians, Deists and Christians, Atheists and both, have attracted my Attention, whenever the singular Life I have lead would admit, to all these questions. The History of this little Village of Quincy, if it were worth recording would explain to you, how this happened. I think, I can now say I have read away Bigotry, if not Enthusiasm.

—Letter to Thomas Jefferson
July 13, 1813

IT APPEARS TO ME the great Principle of the Hebrews was the Fear of God; that of the Gentiles , Honour the Gods, that of Christians, the Love of God.

—Letter to Thomas Jefferson
October 4, 1813

THE PRIESTHOOD HAVE, in all ancient nations, nearly monopolized learning....And, even since the Reformation, when or where has existed a Protestant or dissenting sect who would tolerate A FREE INQUIRY? The blackest billingsgate, the most ungentlemanly insolence, the most yahooish brutality is patiently endured, countenanced, propagated, and applauded. But touch a solemn truth in collision with a dogma or a sect, though capable of the clearest proof, and you will soon find you have disturbed a nest, and the hornets will swam about your legs and hands, and fly into your face and eyes.

—*Letter to John Taylor*
1814

YOU WILL PERCEIVE, by these figures that I have been looking into Oriental History and Hindoo religion. I have read Voyages and travels and every thing I could collect, and the last is Priestleys "Comparison of the Institution of Moses, with those of the Hindoos and other ancient Nations."

—*Letter to Thomas Jefferson*
March 3, 1814

THE TEN COMMANDMENTS and The Sermon on the Mount contain my Religion.

—*Letter to Thomas Jefferson*
November 4, 1816

LET THE HUMAN MIND LOOSE. It must be loose. It will be loose. Superstition and dogmatism cannot confine it.

—Letter to John Quincy Adams
November 13, 1816

AS I UNDERSTAND THE CHRISTIAN RELIGION, it was, and is, a revelation. But how has it happened that millions of fables, tales, legends, have been blended with both Jewish and Christian revelation that have made them the most bloody religion that ever existed?

—Letter to Francis van der Kamp
December 27, 1816

DO YOU RECOLLECT, or have you ever attended to the ecclesiastical Strifes in Maryland, Pensilvania, New York and every part of New England? What a mercy it is that these People cannot whip and crop, and pillory and roast, *as yet,* in the United States. If they could, they would.

—Letter to Thomas Jefferson
May 18, 1817

THAT YOU AND I SHALL MEET IN A BETTER WORLD, I have no more doubt than we now exist on the same globe. If my natural reason did not convince me of this, Cicero's dream of Scipio, and his essays on friendship and old age, would have been sufficient for the purpose. But Jesus has taught us, that a future state is a social state, when he promised to prepare places in his father's house of mant mansions for his disciples.

—Letter to Samuel Miller
July 8, 1820

ADAMS ON
FRIENDS AND FAMILY

John Adams and Abigail Smith Adams were married in 1764. They had six children, four of whom predeceased them—Elizabeth and Susanna died as children, Charles died in 1800 at the age of thirty, and Abigail (Nabby) died in 1813 at the age of forty-eight. Of the two who outlived them, John Quincy went on to become a diplomat and the sixth president of the United States, and Thomas Boylston had a modest political career, serving as his brother's secretary during a diplomatic assignment before returning home to settle in Quincy and serve in the Massachusetts legislature. John and Abigail had fifteen grandchildren, a dozen of whom lived into adulthood.

Since John and Abigail were separated for long periods of time, their correspondence, often addressed "to my dearest friend," reveals their love, activities, and partnership. Abigail Adams died in October 1818, leaving John a grieving widower.

OH MY DEAR GIRL, I thank Heaven that another Fortnight will restore you to me—after so long a separation. My soul and Body have both been thrown into Disorder, by your Absence, and a Month or two more would make me the most insufferable Cynick, in the world. I see nothing but Faults, Follies, Frailties and Defects in any Body, lately. People have lost all their good Properties or I my Justice, or Discernment.

—*Letter to Abigail Adams*
September 30, 1764

I AM SO IDLE, that I have not had an easy Moment, without my Pen in my Hand. My time might have improved to some purpose, in mowing Grass, raking Hay, or hoeing Corn, weeding Carrots, picking or shelling Peas. Much better should I have been employed in schooling my Children, in teaching them to write, cypher, Latin, French, English and Greek.

—Letter to Abigail Adams
July 1, 1774

I WANT TO HEAR YOU think or to see your thoughts. The conclusion of your letter makes my heart throb more than a cannonade would. You bid me burn your letters. But I must forget you first.

—Letter to Abigail Adams
April 28, 1776

IT IS A CRUEL REFLECTION, which very often comes across me, that I should be separated so far, from those Babes, whose Education And Welfare lies so near my Heart. But greater Misfortunes than these, must not divert Us from superiour Duties.

—Letter to Abigail Adams
May 22, 1776

DR. FRANKLIN, one of my colleagues, is so generally known that I shall not attempt a sketch of his character at present. That he was a great genius, a great wit, a great humorist, a great satirist, and a great politician, is certain. That he was a great philosopher, a great moralist, and a great statesman, is more questionable.

—Diary of John Adams
June 7, 1778

MAY HEAVEN PERMIT YOU and me to enjoy the cool Evening of Life, in Tranquility, undisturbed by the Care of Politicks or War—and above all with the sweetest of all Reflections that neither Ambition nor Vanity, nor Avarice, nor Malice nor Envy nor Revenge, nor Fear nor any base Motive, or sordid Passion through the whole Course of this Mighty Revolution, and the rapid impetuous Course of great and terrible Events that have attended it, have drawn Us aside from the Line of our Duty and the Dictates of our Consciences! Let Us have Ambition enough to keep our Simplicity, or Frugality and our Integrity and transmit these Virtues as the fairest of Inheritances to our Children.

—*Letter to Abigail Adams*
June 17, 1780

I SHALL LOOSE ALL OPPORTUNITY of being a man of Importance in the World by being away from home, as well as all the Pleasures of Life: for I never shall enjoy any, any where except at the Foot of Pens hill—When Oh When shall I see the Beauties of that rugged Mountain!

—*Letter to Abigail Adams*
September 25, 1780

FOR MERCY SAKE stop all my Wine but the Bourdeaux and Madeira, and Frontenac. And stop my order to Rouen for 500 Additional Bottles. I shall be ruined, for each Minister is not permitted to import more than 5 or 600 Bottles which will not more than cover what I have at the Hague which is very rich wine and my Madeira Frontenac and Bourdeaux at Auteuil.

—*Letter to Thomas Jefferson*
June 7, 1785

I AM EXTREMELY SORRY, that you could not come for your Daughter in Person, and that we are obliged to part with her so soon. In my Life I never saw a more charming Child. Accept of my Thanks, for the Pamphlets and Arrets.—Tell Mazzei, he cannot conceive what an Italian I am become.—I read nothing else, and if he writes to me it must be in that Language: but he must remember to make his Letters, so plain, that I can see them. In writing English he is obliged to write so slow that his Characters are visible; but in Italian such is the Rapidity of his Eloquence, that I must get a Solar Microscope, if he is not upon his guard. You too, write Italian, and if you like it, you will oblige me: but I am not yet presumptuous enough to write a Line in any Thing but rugged American.

—*Letter to Thomas Jefferson*
July 10, 1787

YOU AND I ARE NOW ENTERING ON A NEW SCENE, which will be the most difficult, and least agreable of any in our Lives. I hope the burthen will be lighter to both of Us, when We come together.

—*Letter to Abigail Adams*
May 4, 1797

MY LITTLE BARK HAS BEEN OVERSETT in a squall of thunder and lightening and hail attended with a strong smell of sulphur.

—*Letter to Thomas Boylston Adams*
December 17, 1800

THE AFFLICTION IN MY FAMILY from the melancholy death of a once beloved son [Charles] has been very great, and has required the consolation of religion, as well as philosophy, to enable me to support it.

—*Letter to François Adriaan van der Kemp*
December 28, 1800

I LIVE ALSO WITH MY FAMILY in a rural, solitary place of retirement, after an uninterrupted toil of six-and-twenty years in the service of the public. Like you also I preserve the love, the doctrines, and the independence of true liberty.

—*Letter to Marquis de Lafayette*
April 6, 1801

I PASSED THE SUMMER OF 1764 in attending Court and pursuing my Studies, with some Amusement on my little farm, to which I was frequently making additions, till the fall when, on the 25th of October, I was married to Miss Smith, a daughter of the Rev. William Smith, a Minister of Weymouth, Granddaughter of the Honorable John Quincy Esquire of Braintree, a connection which has been the source of all my felicity.

—*Autobiography of John Adams*
1802–1807

MY LIFE FOR THE LAST EIGHT YEARS has been spent in the bosom of my family, surrounded by my children and grandchildren; on my farm, in my garden and library.

—*Letter to Skelton Jones*
March 11, 1809

WHEN I WENT HOME TO MY FAMILY IN MAY, 1770, from the town meeting in Boston, which was the first I had ever attended, and where I had been chosen in my absence, without any solicitation, one of their representatives, I said to my wife, "I have accepted a seat in the House of Representatives, and thereby have consented to my own ruin, to your ruin, and to the ruin of our children. I give you this warning, that you may prepare your mind for your fate." She burst into tears, but instantly cried out in a transport of magnanimity, "Well, I am willing in this cause to run all risks with you, and be ruined with you, if you are ruined." These were times, my friend, in Boston which tried women's souls as well as men's.

—Letter to Benjamin Rush
April 12, 1809

PARENTS MUST HAVE THEIR TRIALS. I am now experiencing another. My oldest son sailed on Saturday, the 5th of this month, for St. Petersburg with his family. The separation was like tearing me to pieces. A more dutiful and affectionate son there cannot be. His society was always a cordial and a consolation under all circumstances. I can only pray for his safety and success.

—Letter to Benjamin Rush
August 7, 1809

YOUR LETTER TOUCHES MY HEART. Oh, that I may always be able to say to my grandsons, "You have learned much and behave well, my lads, Go on and improve in everything worthy...I had rather you should be worthy possessors of one thousand pounds honestly acquired by your own labor and industry, than of ten millions by banks and tricks. I should rather you be worthy shoemakers than secretaries of states or treasury acquired by libels in newspapers. I had rather you be worthy makers of brooms and baskets than unworthy presidents of the United States procured by intrigue, factious slander and corruption."

—Letter to John Adams Smith
February 2, 1812

THE BITTERNESS OF DEATH IS PAST. The grim spider so terrible to human nature has no sting left for me.

—Letter to John Quincy Adams
November 10, 1818

MY DEAR SON, Never did I feel so much solemnity as upon this occasion. The multitude of my thoughts, and the intensity of my feelings are too much for a mind like mine, in its ninetieth year. May the blessing of God Almighty continue to protect you to the end of your life, as it has heretofore protected you in so remarkable a manner from your cradle! I offer the same prayer for your lady and your family, and am your affectionate father.

—Letter to John Quincy Adams
February 18, 1826

Retirement and Correspondence with Thomas Jefferson

John Adams and Thomas Jefferson were colleagues from 1775 until 1795 and shared experiences in Philadelphia, London, and Paris. Then they became competitors and adversaries in the elections of 1796 and 1800, and their correspondence and friendship fell dormant. John Adams retired to Quincy in 1801. When Thomas Jefferson left the presidency in March 1809 and returned to Monticello, he was almost sixty-six and Adams was seventy-three. Thanks to the encouragement of Benjamin Rush, the two men resumed contact and their friendship until their deaths on July 4, 1826. At that time, Adams was almost ninety-one and Jefferson was eighty-three. Their correspondence is one of the great treasures in US history. There are 333 letters between Adams and Jefferson and another 45 between Thomas Jefferson and Abigail Adams. In this section there are quotes from letters that John Adams wrote to Thomas Jefferson during their retirement. In the book Thomas Jefferson: In His Own Words, *there are selections from Thomas Jefferson to Adams written during the same time frame.*

HAD YOU READ THE PAPERS INCLOSED they might have given you a moment of Melancholly or at least of Sympathy with a mourning Father. They relate wholly to the Funeral of a Son who was once the delight of my Eyes and a darling of my heart, cutt off in the flower of his days, amidst very flattering Prospects by causes which have been the greatest Grief of my heart and the deepest affliction of my Life. It is not possible that any thing of the kind should happen to you, and I sincerely wish you may never experience any thing in any degree resembling it.

This part of the Union is in a state of perfect Tranquility and I See nothing to obscure your prospect of a quiet and prosperous Administration, which I heartily wish you. With great respect I have the honor to be Sir your most obedient and very humble Servant.

—Letter to Thomas Jefferson
March 24, 1801

I HAVE READ THUCIDIDES AND TACITUS, so often, and at such distant Periods of my Life, that elegant, profound and enchanting as is their Style, I am weary of them. When I read them I seem to be only reaching the History of my own Times and my own Life. I am heartily weary of both; i.e. of recollecting the History of both: for I am not weary of Living. Whatever a peevish Patriarch might say, I have never yet seen the day in which I could say I have had no Pleasure; or that I have had more Pain than Pleasure...

I walk every fair day, sometimes 3 or 4 miles. Ride now and then but very rarely more than ten or fifteen Miles. But I have a Complaint that Nothing but the Ground can cure, that is the Palsy; a kind of Paralytic Affection of the Nerves, which makes my hands tremble, and renders it difficult to write at all and impossible to write well.

I have the Start of you in Age by at least ten Years: but you are advanced to the Rank of a Great Grandfather before me. Of 13 Grand Children I have two, William and John Smith, and three Girls, Caroline Smith, Susanna and Abigail Adams, who might have made me Great Grand Children enough. But they are not likely to employ their Talents very soon. They are all good Boys and Girls however, and are the solace of my Age. I cordially reciprocate your Professions of Esteem and Respect. Madam joins and sends her kind Regards to your Daughter and your Grand Children as well as to yourself.

—Letter to Thomas Jefferson
February 3, 1812

BUT MY LIFE HAS BEEN TOO TRIFLING and my Actions too insignificant for me to write or the Public to read. In my wandering romantic Life, with my incessant *Res angusta Domi,* and my numerous unfortunate Family, of Children and Grand Children without the honour, which you have attained of being a great grandfather, tho' I have a near prospect of it; it has been impossible for me to pursue such Inquiries with any thing like Learning.

—Letter to Thomas Jefferson
May 29, 1813

I RECEIVED YESTERDAY YOUR FAVOUR of may 27th. I lament with you the loss of Rush. I know of no Character living or dead, who has done more real good in America. Robert Treat Paine still lives, at 83 or 84, alert drol and witty though deaf. Floyd I believe, yet remains, Paine must be very great; Philosopher and Christian; to live under the Afflictions of his Family.

—Letter to Thomas Jefferson
June 11, 1813

MY FRIEND! You and I have passed our Lives, in serious Times. I know not whether we have seen any moments more serious than the present. The Northern States are now retaliating, upon the Southern States their conduct from 1797 to 1800. It is a mortification to me to see how servile Mimicks they are.

—Letter to Thomas Jefferson
July 3, 1813

You and I ought not to die, before We have explained our-selves to each other.

—Letter to Thomas Jefferson
July 15, 1813

The Nations of Europe, appeared to me, when I was among them, from the beginning of 1778, to 1785 i.e. to the commencement of the Troubles in France, to be advancing by slow but sure Steps towards an Amelioration of the condition of Man, in Religion and Government, in Liberty, Equality, Fraternity, Knowledge Civilization and Humanity.

—Letter to Thomas Jefferson
July 15, 1813

This World is a mixture of the Sublime and the beautiful, the base and contemptible, the whimsical and ridiculous. (According to our narrow Sense; and triffling Feelings). It is a Riddle and an Enigma.

—Letter to Thomas Jefferson
September 15, 1813

As long as Property exists, it will accumulate in Individuals and Families. As long as marriage exists, Knowledge, Property and Influence will accumulate in Families.

—Letter to Thomas Jefferson
July 16, 1814

EDUCATION! OH EDUCATION! The greatest Grief of my heart, and the greatest Affliction of my Life! To my mortification I must confess, that I have never closely thought, or very deliberately reflected upon the Subject, which never occurs to me now, without producing a deep Sigh, an heavy groan and sometimes Tears. My cruel Destiny seperated me from my Children, allmost continually from their Birth to their Manhood. I was compelled to leave them to the ordinary routine of reading writing and Latin School, Accademy and Colledge. John alone was much with me, and he, but occasionally. If I venture to give you any thoughts at all, they must be very crude.

—Letter to Thomas Jefferson
July 16, 1814

THE QUESTION BEFORE THE HUMAN RACE is, Whether the God of nature shall govern the World by his own laws, or Whether Priests and Kings shall rule it by fictitious Miracles? Or, in other Words, whether Authority is originally in the People?

—Letter to Thomas Jefferson
June 20, 1815

WHO SHALL WRITE THE HISTORY of the American revolution? Who can write it? Who will ever be able to write it? The most essential documents, the debates and deliberations in Congress from 1774 to 1783 were all in secret, and are now lost forever.

—Letter to Thomas Jefferson
July 30, 1815

THE FUND[A]MENTAL ARTICLE of my political Creed is that Despotism, or unlimited Sovereignty, or absolute Power is the same in a Majority of a popular Assembly, an Aristocratical Counsel, an Oligarchical Junto and a single Emperor.

—Letter to Thomas Jefferson
November 13, 1815

AS TO THE HISTORY OF THE REVOLUTION, my Ideas may be peculiar, perhaps singular. What do We Mean by the Revolution? The War? That was no part of the Revolution. It was only an Effect and Consequence of it.

—Letter to Thomas Jefferson
August 24, 1815

WOULD YOU GO BACK TO YOUR CRADLE and live over again Your 70 Years? I believe You would return me a New England Answer, by asking me another question "Would you live your 80 Years over again?"...I have lately lived over again, in part, from 1753, when I was junior Sophister at Colledge till 1769 when I was digging in the Mines, as a Barrister at Law, for Silver and gold, in the Town of Boston; and got as much of the shining dross for my labour as my Utmost Avarice at that time craved...When You asked my Opinion of a University, it would have been easy to

Advise Mathematicks, Experimental Phylosophy, Natural History, Chemistry and Astronomy, Geography and the Fine Arts, to the Exclusion of Ontology, Metaphysicks, and Theology. But knowing the eager Impatience of the human Mind to search into Eternity and Infinity, the first Cause and last End of all Things, I thought best to leave it, its Liberty to inquire till it is convinced as I have been these 50 Years that there is but one Being in the Universe, who comprehends it; and our last Resource is Resignation.

—Letter to Thomas Jefferson
March 2, 1816

NOW SIR, FOR MY GRIEFS! The dear Partner of my Life for fifty four Years as a Wife and for many Years more as a Lover, now lies in extremis, forbidden to speak or be spoken to…The human life is a bubble, no matter how soon it breaks. If it I, as I firmly believe, an immortal existence, we ought patiently to wait the instructions of the great teacher.

—Letter to Thomas Jefferson
October 20, 1818

I KNOW NOT HOW TO PROVE physically that We shall meet and know each other in a future State; Nor does Revelation, as I can find give Us any possitive Assurance of such a felicity. My reasons for believing it, as I do, most undoubtingly, are all moral and divine.

I believe in God and in his Wisdom and Benevolence: and I cannot conceive that such a Being could make such a Species as the human merely to live and die on this Earth. If I did not believe in a future state I should believe in no God.

—Letter to Thomas Jefferson
December 8, 1818

HALF AN HOUR AGO I received, and this moment have heard read for the third or fourth time, the best letter that ever was written by an Octogenearian, dated June the 1st. It is so excellent that I am almost under an invincible temptation to commit a breach of trust by lending it to a printer. My Son, Thomas Boylston, says it would be worth five hundred dollars to any newspaper in Boston, but I dare not betray your confidence...I answer your question, Is Death an Evil? It is not an Evil. It is a blessing to the individual, and to the world. Yet we ought not to wish for it till life becomes insupportable; we must wait the pleasure and convenience of this great teacher. Winter is as terrible to me, as to you.

—Letter to Thomas Jefferson
June 11, 1822

THE PRESIDENTIAL ELECTION has given me less anxiety than I, myself could have imagined. The next administration will be a troublesome one to whomso-ever it falls. And our John has been too much worn to contend much longer with conflicting factions. I call him our John, because when you was at Cul de sac at Paris, he appeared to me to be almost as much your boy as mine. I have often speculated upon the consequences that would have ensued from my takeing your advice, to send him to William and Mary College in Virginia for an Education.

—Letter to Thomas Jefferson
January 22, 1825

Acknowledgments

The Adams Family Papers, from which much of this material was selected, is among the best resources in US history. The papers have been housed at the Massachusetts Historical Society since 1902, and the first major collection of these papers was edited by Charles Francis Adams and published in 1850 to 1856. Beginning in 1961, a newer edition has been under way, initially under the guidance of L. H. Butterfield. We are grateful to the Massachusetts Historical Society, to C. James Taylor, editor in chief of the Adams papers, who wrote an introduction to this book, and to Dennis Fiori, Peter Drummey, and Conrad Wright.

John Adams established a wonderful library that was extensively used during his lifetime and whose books were read by many of his descendants. Since 1894 the Adams Library has resided at the Boston Public Library. We would like to offer our thanks to Beth Prindle, who organized an exhibit from the Adams Library collection, introduced us to many of John Adams's books, organized a traveling exhibit on John Adams, and also wrote an introduction to this book.

Thanks also to the authors of the biographies listed in the bibliography, as well as to the Boston Public Library and the Denver Public Library. Finally, thanks most of all to the Adams family, which for generations has served the United States in so many ways.

List of Correspondents

Abigail Smith Adams
  wife

John Quincy Adams
  eldest son, sixth US president

Samuel Adams
  cousin, Massachusetts governor

Thomas Boylston Adams
  youngest son

William Crawford
  presidential candidate in 1828

Samuel Dexter
  secretary of war

Benjamin Franklin
  statesman, printer, scientist

Horatio Gates
  Continental Army general

Moses Gill
  friend, lieutenant governor of Massachusetts

Nathanael Greene
  Continental Army general

Patrick Henry
  Revolution leader, Virginia governor

Jonathan Jackson
  Massachusetts representative to Congress

Thomas Jefferson
  third US president

Skelton Jones
  author, *History of Virginia*

Rufous King
  Massachusetts representative to Congress

Henry Knox
  Continental Army general

Marquis de Lafayette
  French reformer, Continental Army general

James Madison
  fourth US president

James Monroe
  fifth US president

John Marshall
  secretary of state, chief justice of the Supreme Court

Thomas McKean
  Pennsylvania chief justice

Samuel Miller
  professor

Hezekiah Niles
  editor, *Weekly Register*

Dr. Richard Price
  English radical

Josiah Quincy III
    Massachusetts friend, son of Boston's mayor

Benjamin Rush
    physician, signer of the Declaration of Independence

Richard Rush
    Benjamin Rush's son, attorney general,
    minister to Great Britain

Jonathan Sewall
    lawyer, friend, exiled to England

John Adams Smith
    grandson

William Smith
    son-in-law

John Taylor
    political writer, agriculturist

J. H. Tiffany
    correspondent

William Tudor
    fellow law student

François Adriaan van der Kemp
    friend, Dutch Patriot movement leader

Benjamin Vaughan
    British diplomat

James Warren
    state representative from Weymouth

Mercy Otis Warren
    friend, author

George Washington
    first US president

Benjamin Waterhouse
    Massachusetts physician

BIBLIOGRAPHY

ORIGINAL DOCUMENTS

Adams Family Papers, Massachusetts Historical Society

Abigail Adams Papers, Massachusetts Historical Society

Abigail Adams Papers, American Antiquarian Society

A Defence of the Constitutions of Government of the United States of America. Philadelphia: Hall and Sellers, 1787. Reprint, 1971.

Catalogue of the John Adams Library in the Public Library of the City of Boston. Boston: Boston Trustees, 1917.

Adams, John. *History of the Dispute with America, From Its Origin, In 1754 to the Present Time.* London: J. Stockdale, 1784. Reprint, Boston: Hews and Gross, 1819.

The Correspondence of John Adams. Baltimore, MA: H. Niles, 1809.

COLLECTIONS OF JOHN ADAMS'S WRITINGS

Adams, Charles Francis, ed. *Correspondence of John Adams and Mercy Warren.* Boston: Massachusetts Historical Society, 1878. Reprint, New York: Arno Press, 1972.

————. *Familiar Letters of John Adams and His Wife Abigail during the Revolution.* Freeport: Books for Libraries Press, 1970.

———. *Letters of John Adams, Addressed to His Wife.* Boston: C. C. Little and J. Brown, 1841.

———. *The Works of John Adams.* 10 vols. Boston: Little Brown, 1850–1856.

Butterfield, L. H. *The Book of Abigail and John.* Cambridge: Harvard Univ. Press, 1975. Reprint, Boston: Northeastern Univ. Press, 2002.

Butterfield, L. H., et al., eds. *Adams Family Correspondence.* Vol. 1–8. Cambridge: Harvard Univ. Press, 1963–.

———. *Diary and Autobiography of John Adams.* Vol. 1–4. Cambridge, NJ: Harvard Univ. Press, 1961.

———. *The Earliest Diary of John Adams.* Cambridge: Harvard Univ. Press, 1966.

Cappon, Lester J., ed. *The Adams-Jefferson Letters.* Chapel Hill: Univ. of North Carolina, 1959. Reprint, 1988.

Diggins, John Patrick, ed. *The Portable John Adams.* New York: Penguin Classics, 2004.

Ford, Worthington Chauncy, ed. *Statesman and Friend: Correspondence of John Adams and Benjamin Waterhouse.* Boston: Little Brown, 1927.

Hogan, Margaret A., and C. James Taylor, eds. *My Dearest Friend: Letters of Abigail and John Adams.* Cambridge: Harvard Univ. Press, 2007.

Koch, Adrienne, and William Peden, eds. *The Selected Writings of John and John Quincy Adams.* New York: Knopf, 1946.

Taylor, Robert, et al., eds. *Papers of John Adams.* Vol. 1–13. Cambridge: Harvard Univ. Press, 1983–.

Books on John Adams

Adams, Henry. *History of the United States during the Administration of Thomas Jefferson*. New York: Scribners, 1889. Reprint, New York: Library of America, 1986.

Adams, James Truslow. *The Adams Family*. Boston: Little, Brown, 1930.

———. *Revolutionary New England, 1691-1776*. Boston: Atlantic Monthly Press, 1923.

Akers, Charles W. *Abigail Adams: An American Woman*. Boston: Little, Brown, 1980.

Allison, John Murray. *Adams and Jefferson: The Story of a Friendship*. Norman: Univ. of Oklahoma, 1966.

Bailyn, Bernard. *Faces of Revolution: Personalities and Themes in the Struggle for American Independence*. New York: Knopf, 1990.

———. *The People of British North America*. New York: Vintage, 1986.

Bowen, Catharine Drinker. *John Adams and the American Revolution*. Boston: Little Brown, 1950.

Brookheiser, Richard. *America's First Dynasty: The Adamses, 1735-1918*. New York: The Free Press, 2002.

Brown, Ralph Adams. *The Presidency of John Adams*. Lawrence: Univ. Press of Kansas, 1975.

Chinard, Gilbert. *Honest John Adams*. Boston: Little Brown, 1923.

Diggins, John P. *John Adams*. New York: Times Books, 2003.

Elkins, Stanley, and Eric McKitrick. *The Age of Federalism*. New York: Oxford Univ. Press, 1993.

Ellis, Joseph J. *Founding Brothers: The Revolutionary Generation.* New York: Knopf, 2000.

———. *Passionate Sage.* New York: Norton, 1993.

Ferling, John E. *John Adams: A Life.* Chattanooga: Univ. of Tennessee, 1992.

———. *Setting the World Ablaze: Washington, Adams, Jefferson and the American Revolution.* New York: Oxford Univ. Press, 2000.

Fiske, John R. *The American Revolution.* 2 vols. Boston: Riverside Press, 1891.

Fliegelman, Jay. *Declaring Independence.* Stanford, CA: Stanford Univ. Press, 1993.

Forbes, Esther. *Paul Revere and the World He Lived In.* Boston: Houghton, Mifflin, 1942.

Grant, James. *John Adams: Party of One.* New York: Farrar, Straus, and Giroux, 2005.

Handlin, Oscar, and Lillian Handlin. *A Restless People: Americans in Rebellion, 1770–1787.* Garden City, NY: Doubleday, 1982.

Haraszti, Zoltan. *John Adams and the Prophets of Power.* Cambridge, MA: Harvard Univ. Press, 1952.

Holfstadter, Richard. *The American Political Tradition and the Men Who Made It.* New York: Knopf, 1948.

Howe, John R. *The Changing Political Thought of John Adams.* Princeton, NJ: Princeton Univ. Press, 1966.

Levin, Phyllis Lee. *Abigail Adams: A Biography.* New York: St. Martin's Press, 1987.

Lodge, Henry Cabot. *Alexander Hamilton.* Boston: Houghton Mifflin, 1882.

———. *Story of Revolution.* Boston: Riverside Press, 1898.

Malone, Dumas. *Jefferson and His Time.* 6 vols. Boston: Little, Brown, 1948–1981.

McCullough, David. *1776.* New York: Simon and Schuster, 2005.

———. *John Adams.* New York: Simon and Schuster, 2001.

Miller, Perry. *The New England Mind in the Seventeenth Century.* Cambridge, MA: Harvard Univ. Press, 1939.

Morgan, Edmund S. *The Birth of the Republic, 1763–1789.* Chicago: Univ. of Chicago Press, 1992.

———. *The Meaning of Independence.* New York: Norton, 1976.

Nagel, Paul C. *The Adams Women.* New York: Oxford Univ. Press, 1987.

———. *Descent from Glory.* New York: Oxford, 1983.

———. *John Quincy Adams.* New York: Knopf, 1997.

Osborne, Angela. *Abigail Adams.* New York: Chelsea House, 1989.

Peterson, Merill. *Adams and Jefferson: A Revolutionary Dialog.* New York: Oxford Univ. Press, 1976.

Rosenfeld, Richard. *American Aurora.* New York: St. Martin's, 1997.

Ryerson, Richard Alan, ed. *John Adams and the Founding of the Republic.* Boston: Massachusetts Historical Society, 2001.

Schulz, John A., and Douglass Adair. *The Spur of Fame: Dialogues of John Adams and Benjamin Rush, 1805–1813.* San Marino, CA: The Huntington Library, 1966. Reprint, 2000.

Shaw, Peter. *The Character of John Adams.* New York: Norton, 1976.

Sheppard, Jack. *The Adams Chronicles: Four Generations of Greatness.* Boston:
    Little Brown, 1976.

Smith, Page. *John Adams.* 2 vols. Garden City, NY: Doubleday, 1962.

van der Linden, Frank. *The Turning Point: Jefferson's Battle for the Presidency.*
    Golden, CO: Fulcrum Publishing, 2000.

Vidal, Gore. *Inventing a Nation: Washington, Adams, Jefferson.* New Haven, CT:
    Yale Univ. Press, 2003.

Warren, Mercy Otis. *History of the Rise, Progress, and Termination of the
    American Revolution.* Edited by Lester Cohen. Indianapolis: Liberty
    Foundation, 1989.

Wood, Gordon S. *The Creation of the American Republic, 1776–1787.* New York:
    Norton, 1972.

———. *The Radicalization of the American Revolution.* New York: Knopf, 1992.

For more information about our titles and to order a catalog,
please contact us at:

Fulcrum Publishing
4690 Table Mountain Drive, Suite 100
Golden, Colorado 80403
E-mail: info@fulcrumbooks.com
Toll-free: 800-992-2908
Fax: 800-726-7112
www.fulcrumbooks.com

FULCRUM